The Mighty MGs

Graham Robson

The Mighty
MGs

The Twin-Cam, MGC
and MGB GT V8 Stories

MERCIAN MANUALS
BALSALL COMMON
COVENTRY CV7 7EE

British Library Cataloguing in Publication Data

Robson, Graham
    The Mighty MGs: the twin-cam, MGC and MGB GT V8
    stories.
    1. M.G. automobile
    I. Title
    629.2′222   TL215.M2

ISBN 0 9530721 3 4

Published by Mercian Manuals
242 Station Road. Balsall Commom
Coventry CV7 7EE

Contents

Introduction

Let me start by justifying the need for yet another MG title. Among all the previous books written about MG cars, it has always seemed to me that the three most exciting modern MG models have been rather neglected. Now that the traditional MG marque has been killed off by BL Cars, it must surely be the time for the careers of the MGA Twin-Cam, the MGC, and the MGB GT V8—truly, the Mighty MGs—to be chronicled, fully, painstakingly, and accurately, before factory records are either mislaid or destroyed.

This, therefore, is the story of just three cars. Each, in its own way, was quite out of the ordinary by current MG standards, and each sold only in limited numbers. Each model, however, was considerably faster than, and technically quite different from, the mass-market MGs being built at the time, and stood well apart from them. Each, by any contemporary standard, was a Mighty MG.

All three cars, of course, were blessed with a great deal of that indefinable substance called 'character'. This is not to say that they were sensationally successful, and certainly not to state that they were outstandingly better than their principal rivals, but that one could never ignore them, or write them off as boring and insignificant. No doubt there would be BMC or BL financial whizz-kids ready to tell you that all three were financial failures, and production managers to assure you that they always caused administrative disruption at Abingdon. A true MG enthusiast, on the other hand, would probably have more to say about them than about the more numerous MGAs and MGBs.

This book, however, is not meant to re-kindle the 'golden glow' of Mighty MG ownership and worship, while ignoring or suppressing the problems which are known to be associated with each model. It would be quite wrong, for instance, to ignore the engine reliability problems of the original Twin-Cams, the distinctly un-Abingdon-like handling of the MGC, and the pricing problems of the V8. To balance that, of course, I would be failing to present proper history if I neglected the technical merit and outstanding performance of the Twin-Cam, the long-legged cruising gait of the MGC, and the ingenious packaging and sparkling performance of the V8.

I hope, therefore, that this book will be looked on as a chronicle of facts about the Mighty MGs, and not an exercise in wishful thinking. I want people to realise, for instance, that if only the Big Healey had not matured at the same time, then the Abingdon Competitions Department might have developed the Twin-Cam into a world-class competition car. I want to make it clear that the MGC could have been much livelier if only a few of the cost-effective Downton modifications had been applied to the basic 3-litre engine provided by Morris Engines. I also want to emphasise that an MGB-V8 marriage might have been a real commercial success if it had been authorised several years earlier.

As with other books I have prepared about BL cars in recent years, I have been lucky enough to be able to draw on a mass of statistical material now held by BL Heritage, and I repeat my thanks to them in another section of this book. It means that I have been able to provide complete and accurate data regarding the production history of each model, much of which has most certainly never been made available to MG enthusiasts before.

Will there ever be any more Mighty MGs? Alas! Unless there is a radical change of heart at BL Cars, and a phenomenal improvement in their finances, I think not. In which case, we must all try to preserve the stocks of existing models, and enjoy them to the full.

① The Birth of the Twin-Cam

Although the MGA Twin-Cam model was announced in 1958, there are two separate development stories to be considered in the years which led up to the launch: the evolution of the twin overhead camshaft engine itself, and that of the car which eventually received it. In previous MG books it has never been made clear that the two projects were not always inextricably linked, but came together at a rather later stage. Certain known, and authenticated, dates make this quite obvious, however. Although the MGA sports car had been designed (around the old-type Nuffield XPAG/XPEG engine and transmission) in 1952, it was almost immediately shelved. It was not until it was revived in 1954 that the new BMC B-Series engine became a part of the design. The twin-cam engine, on the other hand, started life in 1953 as a paper proposal, sketched out by Gerald Palmer, who was then chief engineer of Morris Motors (Cars Branch) at Cowley, a post which included responsibility for new MG models. At the time, therefore, the only obvious place for the twin-cam engine was in the still secret MG Magnette ZA saloon!

If it were not for the fact that the BMC merger, announced in the winter of 1951/2 and only just beginning to take practical effect, had thrown the entire Austin and Nuffield design and management scene into considerable turmoil, I would have found it very difficult to believe, or understand, the illogical events which took place in the months which followed. However, as I was not merely an observer, but was actually in, or very close to, the motor industry of the day, I can bear witness to the many strange decisions taken by the new BMC management, most of which, I must admit, were taken in the interests of rationalisation. For the MG management team—of whom John Thornley was the most important, and the most notable—it must have been a very difficult time.

Briefly, therefore, I ought to review the way in which the engine itself, and the motor car which it was eventually to power, came into existence, and I ought also to spell out the events which preceded them.

MG had come into existence in the 1920s, as a concern totally and privately owned by William Morris. By 1935 Morris had become Lord Nuffield, and for a variety of practical and financial reasons he decided to create the Nuffield Group from Morris Motors, Wolseley, MG, Morris Commercial, and several other component supply concerns which had grown up with Morris Motors. At that point, the design office at MG's Abingdon works was closed down, and responsibility for new-model development passed to the main Nuffield design office at Cowley. After the end of the Second World War, there was only a tiny development department at Abingdon, which was headed by Syd Enever.

In 1949, Gerald Palmer, who had designed the Jowett Javelin during the war and seen it go into production at Bradford in the years which followed, moved to Cowley to become chief designer of MG and Riley, with an extraordinarily wide brief. Very soon he was not only proposing new Wolseley models as well but was also taking a hand in the styling, as well as the engineering, of the new range of cars. MG (and Syd Enever), however, were not entirely stifled. In 1951 Enever produced a remarkably beautiful *and* aerodynamically efficient body shell for George Phillips's Le Mans MG TD, and early in 1952 he designed an all-new box-section chassis frame to mate with the new style, allowing a much lower driver's seating position to be provided. That, in effect, was the birth of the MGA project, to which I shall return a little later.

In the meantime, great corporate changes had taken place. From the 1920s to the end of the 1940s, the two giants of the still-strong British motor industry were Austin and Morris. Both companies were controlled by the individuals who had given their names to the cars built, and by the late 1930s both the eminent founders had been ennobled—as Lord Austin and Lord Nuffield. One other remarkable character linked the two—Leonard Lord, who had achieved fame and considerable status with Nuffield, quarrelled violently with Lord Nuffield in 1936 and walked out on him, stayed out of the industry for a time, and then joined Austin as the heir apparent in 1938. Lord Austin died in 1941 and immediately after the war Leonard Lord became the guiding genius behind the expansion of Austin.

By 1948 Lord had become convinced that Austin and Morris ought to merge (on his terms, naturally—he was not prepared to become subservient to Lord Nuffield for a second time). But early approaches to Nuffield resulted only in partial co-operation about systems, costing, design, and production methods, which were dissolved in July 1949. The definitive merger proposal was delayed until the end of 1951, and became operational early in 1952. For a few months—theoretically at least—Lord Nuffield was the supremo of the new British Motor Corporation, but he could never have been content and, in the autumn of 1952, he retired to become BMC's Honorary President.

Right from the start, Leonard Lord set out on a ruthless course of mechanical rationalisation. He wanted to reduce the cost and complication of building a real *mélange* of Austin, Morris, and Wolseley-type engines and their related transmissions. With Austin nominated as design leaders for new projects (no BMC spokesman ever satisfactorily explained whether the ADO project codes meant *Austin* Drawing Office or *Amalgamated* Drawing Office, although both titles were used in the years which followed), he directed that three new engines should replace all others: the small A-Series engine, based on the unit designed for the 1951 Austin A30, the B-Series, a developed and enlarged version of the Austin A40 1,200cc engine, first seen in 1947, and a new straight six-cylinder engine, to be designed at the Morris Engines Branch factory in Coventry, and intended to use some components common with the B-Series design. There would be A-, B-, and C-Series gearboxes and axles to suit—with some new units actually being designed at the Nuffield office in Cowley.

This policy had an immediate effect on the cars being built, or planned, at MG. In 1952 the MG cars in production were the TD sports car and the YB saloon, both of which used derivations of the XP-Series four-cylinder engine, a Nuffield gearbox, and a Nuffield hypoid bevel axle. All of these had effectively been sentenced to death by the design projects emanating from the BMC merger.

In 1952/3—at which time all MG design work was still controlled from Cowley—Gerald Palmer was told to instal the B-Series engine and transmissions in any MGs which were brewing. In a way, this was very aggravating, because his team had already completed layout work on the Wolseley 4/44 and MG Magnette

ZA duo. The 4/44 was ready, and tooled up, for production too early for the edict to take effect, and went on sale with a single-carburettor version of the old engine, but the ZA Magnette had to be speedily re-designed. There were no immediate plans to update the TD (the all-enveloping design which we now know as the MGA had already been rejected by Leonard Lord, don't forget), so this and the facelifted TF which followed it in the autumn of 1953 were also allowed to continue using the old engine.

In effect, it was the re-design for the Magnette, with a tuned version of the B-Series Austin engine installed, which led directly to the birth and evolution of a twin-cam engine. Gerald Palmer, who was above all a motoring enthusiast first, and a 'corporation man' second, knew not only that John Thornley was itching to get MG back into serious competition—racing in particular—but also that BMC engineers were having difficulty in getting much more than 60bhp, with acceptable reliability, from the 1,489cc B-Series overhead valve engine which was scheduled for use in the ZA Magnette from the autumn of 1953. Somehow or other, therefore, it was Palmer himself who found time to sit down at his drawing board, consider the various alternatives, and scheme out a proposed twin overhead camshaft conversion of the B-Series engine. As drawn up by Palmer, its two lines of valves were symmetrically disposed at an included angle of 90 degrees, and it was intended to use as many as possible of the B-Series engine's existing components.

Several points arise. One was that this was one of the very first attempts to marry a twin-cam head to an existing pushrod overhead-valve cylinder block design (no other sizeable concern had tackled such a job). Another was that there were very few precedents, as the *only* two twin-cam engines currently in any sort of quantity production were being built by Alfa Romeo in Italy, and by Jaguar in Coventry.

Palmer's layout was certainly influenced by these engines, and by the Grand Prix fashion of the day. In 1952/3 the outstanding GP engine was the four-cylinder 2-litre Ferrari unit, which had an included angle of 58 degrees between lines of valves, while those of the Jaguar and the Alfa Romeo were 70 degrees and 90 degrees respectively. Even then, the trend was gradually to reduce the angle between lines of valves (it made the gas-flow characteristics easier to optimise, and it made the head casting itself more compact), so in this respect Palmer's design can be seen as a little behind the times. The Nuffield chief engineer, however, did not pretend to be an engine design specialist, and was happy to turn it over to James Thompson, chief engineer of the Morris Engines Branch, for consideration. But it is important to realise that the general layout proposed by Palmer, including the 'Jaguar-type' inverted bucket style of valve gear operation, was never substantially changed for production units.

An official project to produce a twin-overhead camshaft conversion on the basis of the B-Series engine was approved by George Harriman (BMC's deputy managing director—and Leonard Lord's right-hand man) early in 1953, and several sources confirm that work began in March 1953. Incidentally, in spite of what might have been suggested in other books, this twin-cam engine was definitely not originally suggested by John Thornley, though it is true to say that Thornley embraced its possibilities just as soon as he heard about its existence and knew that the B-Series engine would have to be fitted into the next MG sports car. His reasoning was simple, and very straightforward:

> We wanted the engine purely for competitions. . . . We aimed at a limited market. We wanted to make 25 a week. Then we could steer them around to those enthusiastic people who would know how to handle them throughout the world.

James Thompson, ably assisted by his development chief in Coventry, Eddie Maher (who had originally made his reputation with Riley in the 1930s when that firm was still independent and still actively involved in motor racing), set about productionising Palmer's idea, which was clearly a good one, and after taking advice from Harry Weslake, who had been an Austin Motor Co. consultant for some years and was now retained by BMC, reduced the included valve angle to 80 degrees, not only to make the head a touch narrower, but to tidy up the air-flow possibilities, and to make the combustion process rather more predictable. It was the problem of achieving satisfactory combustion which was to plague the Twin-Cam engine throughout its life, and one which directly led to its demise.

While all this was going on, Leonard Lord indulged in one of his periodic flights of whimsy. He decided that there was nothing to beat the spirit of competition in his new group, and he encouraged the engine designers at Longbridge—the original 'Austin' team—to produce a twin-cam engine of their own. Their brief was more simple than that given to Morris Engines—their design could be unique from end to end, and top to bottom. (One previous source suggests that the Austin engine was also a B-Series 'conversion', but this has never been backed up by any other reference.)

The result of this design competition is now well known. Both engines were revealed to the public in September 1955, a few days before the MG team cars left Abingdon to compete in the Tourist Trophy race at Dundrod in Northern Ireland, when it was intended to run one of each engine in the race alongside a third car fitted with a pushrod B-Series engine in Le Mans race tune. Over the years there has been great confusion as to which engine (or both, or neither) actually raced in the Dundrod TT, for almost every written source differs from its contemporaries. I even made an error myself in another book, and I am now happy to correct it from a most unimpeachable source—by consulting the then Competition Manager of BMC, Marcus Chambers. In a recent letter to me, Marcus states:

> Only one twin-cam engine raced [in the TT]. It was the Morris Engines one. This was because the rev limit on the Longbridge engine was no better than the standard (pushrod) engine. There were also carburettor problems.

The story is quite conclusive, and the fortunes of the team cars in this race are described more fully in Chapter 4. At this point, however, I merely note that the 'Austin' (or 'Longbridge') engine had been developed by a team headed by H. V. Appleby, who had been a junior member of the design group behind the twin-overhead-camshaft single-seater Austin racing car of 1936–9. It has even been suggested, on rather tenuous grounds, that there were superficial similarities between the 1955 1.5-litre Austin 'twin-cam', and the 1936 supercharged 750cc racing unit.

Although the new Morris Engines twin-cam design achieved no success in the Dundrod TT (it is a long and complicated story), it was obviously considered promising enough. The competition between the Austin and Morris camps ceased forthwith, the Austin engine was never seen again and, as far as is known, has not even been preserved for posterity. In spite of the brief

The rebodied MG TD Le Mans car of 1951, ready to race. This Abingdon shot features Alec Hounslow at the wheel, with designer Syd Enever (in suit) alongside him. This car was broken up many years ago (*BL*)

and unsuccessful appearance of the Morris Engines design in the prototype MGA at Dundrod, it was decided that this could form the basis of a new production car, and serious development then got under way.

Which brings me neatly to consideration of the car itself. There is little point in describing the birth and concept of the original MGA in any detail, but I should concentrate on the Twin-Cam model itself. As every MG enthusiast now knows, the MGA story began with the design by Syd Enever of a full-width two-seater sports car body (coded EX172 at Abingdon) for fitment to a race-prepared TD chassis frame, so that *Autosport* photographer George Phillips could have a competitive machine to use at Le Mans in 1951. This style was refined with the help of the Armstrong-Whitworth aeroplane wind tunnel near Coventry, and was very effective at Le Mans, though its effect was partly nullified

15

by the need to seat Phillips or his co-driver on top of, rather than alongside, the main chassis side members.

This irritated Syd Enever considerably, and in February 1952 (with the connivance of, but with no active encouragement from, the Cowley design office) he designed a new and altogether more suitable chassis frame to suit. This frame, and mechanical layout, coded EX175, featured box section side members widely swept outwards around the passenger compartment, and the result was that the seats could be dropped down between the side members and the transmission tunnel, thus reducing the frontal area considerably.

Two prototype frames were purchased from John Thompson Motor Pressings of Wolverhampton, and one was built up into a complete car, powered by a 1,250cc MG TD engine and also using the TD's gearbox and hypoid bevel back axle, and registered HMO 6. The only minor blemish in the entire design was that a bonnet bulge was needed to provide clearance for the rather tall TD engine.

It was such an outstanding car, so 'right' with almost no development, that John Thornley decided to demonstrate it to Leonard Lord, and ask for approval, and funds, for it to be put into production, to replace the traditionally-styled MG TD. However, as he has said on several occasions, 'it was shown to Leonard Lord three days too late', for Lord had already seen the original Healey 100 (which used redundant Austin A90 engines and transmissions, and was therefore a very attractive commercial proposition), had agreed to adopt it as the Austin-Healey 100, and was in no mood to commission yet another BMC sports car project for the time being.

Thornley and Enever, therefore, had to retire hurt for a time. They had to carry out a rushed and not altogether successful face lift on the TD (which resulted in the TF), and in 1953 and 1954 they saw their market leadership not only attacked from within the corporation, by the Big Healey, but also from Standard-Triumph, with the TR2. It was not until June 1954, with MG sports car sales suffering badly, that BMC gave Thornley the go-ahead to develop and put into production the new car—on the basis that it was to use the BMC B-Series engine and transmission, as already fitted to the ZA Magnette saloon. The new project became EX182, and the time-scale (which looked extremely difficult at the time,

After the 1955 Le Mans race, when three pushrod-engined MGA prototypes raced, and two finished, LBL 303, which had taken 17th place, was fitted with full all-weather equipment, windscreen, and a more suitable gearbox and axle ratio, and loaned to *Autocar* for trial. Harold Holt is at the wheel (*Autocar*)

and proved to be impossible in practice to achieve) envisaged that the first production cars would be ready for announcement before June 1955. Body shells were to be supplied by the Morris Bodies Branch in Coventry, chassis frames from John Thompson, and the power train from Austin factories in and around Birmingham.

Before the end of 1954, BMC also decided officially to re-enter motor sport, opened a Competitions Department at Abingdon, and appointed Marcus Chambers as its manager. Rallying was to be a principal activity, but it was also decided to enter a team of MGAs for the Le Mans 24-hour sports car race in June 1955. At first, it was hoped to have production cars on the market by then, but there were delays in completing the body tooling, and the Le

Mans cars had to be called 'prototypes'. One car crashed badly at Le Mans. Nevertheless, as we have seen, the team was also present at Dundrod, for the Tourist Trophy race, and it was there that the twin-cam engines made their first appearance.

The development of the Twin-Cam MGA, therefore, really stems from that first racing appearance, even though the car eventually put on sale to the public was by no means the same car which had raced. In particular, the wheels and the brakes used on production Twin-Cams never made an appearance in public, not even on a competition car, though if Thornley and Marcus Chambers had had their way this would certainly have come to pass.

Two horrifying accidents—one involving an MG team driver, Dick Jacobs, at Le Mans, and one resulting in drivers being killed during the Dundrod Tourist Trophy race—influenced BMC management very much, and following the second of these events it was decided that BMC's future competition effort should be confined to rallying, and to record breaking. Any racing which did take place would have to be financed (or *nominally* financed, at least) by private individuals, or by BMC concessionaires in the countries involved overseas.

This decision rather threw MG's planning out of synchronisation, as for the 1956 season not only had they wanted to use prototype twin-cam engines in relatively standard MGA models, but they also had two rather specialised project cars—EX183 and EX186—under consideration. EX183 combined a new tubular-chassis design under the skin of a light-alloy look-alike MGA body with a twin-cam engine, while EX186 used a relatively standard MGA frame (with De Dion rear suspension) and a twin-cam engine with an all-new body style. In each case, MG were thinking of using more advanced wheel and braking equipment—centre-lock disc wheels looking superficially like those by the racing Jaguar D-Types of 1954 and 1955, allied to four-wheel Dunlop disc brakes. It was this configuration, of course, which was eventually to be adopted for the production Twin-Cam, but, as it happened, any racing experience which might have assisted the production-car design engineers was lost, and all prototype testing had to be carried out on normal road cars.

This is, however, an appropriate place to analyse why these 'corners' were chosen in favour of the MGA's standard equipment. The ordinary MGA, of course, was offered only with drum

For the Tourist Trophy Race of 1955, one of the lightweight Le Mans MGAs was fitted with Girling front-wheel disc brakes, reprofiled front wings, Riley Pathfinder small-diameter auxiliary 'headlamps', and a prototype Morris Engines Twin-Cam engine of 1,489cc. The car was forced to retire when hastily made inlet manifolds developed hair-line cracks, air leaks, and ruined the carburation (*BL*)

brakes at front and rear (in the autumn of 1955, when it was revealed, Europe's only—brand-new—production car to have disc brakes was the very advanced Citroen DS19 saloon), and the choice of pressed-steel bolt-on disc wheels, or centre-lock wire-spoke wheels. Neither the existing brakes, nor the choice of wheels, was considered to be up to the job demanded of them for a twin-cam-equipped road car.

The steel disc wheels were—or could be made—strong enough, but it was thought that most enthusiasts (particularly those interested in racing or rallying their cars, and they were likely to form the majority of Twin-Cam customers) would want some sort of knock-off, centre-lock wheels. Conventional wire-spoke wheels not only tended to get dirty remarkably quickly, but they were not laterally rigid, and often began to suffer from loose or broken spokes at quite low mileages.

Fortunately for MG, the newly designed centre-lock Dunlop disc wheels had been designed specifically for Jaguar and the D-Type in 1953/4, and had proved to combine the merits of both established types of wheel. (At the time, it should be recalled, no cast-alloy wheel was available at a commercially acceptable price.) The wheels used by Jaguar featured light-alloy centre pressings, but these would have been too expensive for MG to offer for a road car, so it was decided to use pressed-steel centres, which were perhaps a little heavier but offered considerably better value for money.

The choice of brakes was more complex. MG, like Jaguar, Austin-Healey and Triumph, were faced at this time with the fact that three British concerns—Dunlop, Girling and Lockheed—were all nearly ready to offer disc-brake equipment for road cars, and all were looking for business. As far as MG were concerned, a strictly commercial choice between these firms had to be coloured by the fact that they had chosen Lockheed drum brakes for

HMO 6 was the first real prototype of the MGA, built in 1952, but fitted with MG TD engine, gearbox, and back-axle assemblies. Like UMG 400, it was broken up many years ago. The bonnet bulge was needed to clear the rocker cover of the TD's Type XPAG engine (*BL*)

the MGA production car when it was introduced in 1955. Further complications were that Dunlop were pushing ahead with four-disc brake installations whereas Girling and Lockheed were both concentrating on front disc/rear drum systems, and that Lockheed development was lagging somewhat behind the other concerns.

The agony of choice which faced manufacturers like MG was indicated by the fact that the 1955 Le Mans Triumph TR2s ran with two different types of disc-brake installation (one car used Dunlop, and two others used Girling brakes), that MG used Girling front disc brakes on the Twin-Cam car entered for the 1955 Tourist Trophy race, that it was Dunlop who gained all the early publicity when their brakes were used on C-Type and D-Type Jaguars, and that it was Girling who gained the contract to brake the 1957-model Triumph TR3, which made its public debut in October 1956.

MG, having analysed all this information, having seen the way in which the makers of true performance cars—like Jaguar and Jensen—chose the four-wheel Dunlop disc braking system, and having decided that this was the 'purest', in engineering terms,

layout, settled on the Dunlop layout, and became only the third *quantity-production* manufacturer in Britain to offer disc brakes as standard. Jaguar and Triumph were the other two concerns which beat MG to the post. (Incidentally, when it became time to offer disc brakes on the MGA 1600, and on the Austin-Healey 3000, both of which were assembled at Abingdon in 1959, Lockheed brakes were chosen for the MGA and Girling brakes for the Big Healey!)

While all this was going on, the original twin overhead camshaft engine was being developed, and refined, into a machine suitable and capable of relatively limited quantity production. From time to time (as detailed in Chapter 4), prototype units appeared once again in MG record cars, but behind the scenes at the Morris Engines factory in Coventry efforts were being made to turn the basic unit into a reliable machine, for high-mileage road use.

All the initial testing and development was of 1,489cc engines — on the assumption that this was not only the size used in the pushrod-engined MGA and the Magnette saloon but in almost every other B-Series equipped BMC car, and also on the assumption that the cylinder block to be used for the Twin-Cam should, and could, be machined on existing transfer machinery at Longbridge. It was not long, however, before it became necessary to move the location of the cylinder-head holding-down studs, to make modifications connected with the removal of the distributor from its position on the offside of the cylinder block to one on the front cover of the Twin-Cam, to make changes . . . no, the list is too long to detail here. Suffice it to say that the production cylinder block was already looking very non-standard (and in need of special machining operations before being ready for assembly) even before the decision was taken to enlarge the engine itself, from 1,489cc to 1,588cc.

This came at quite a late stage. At one point it had been hoped to introduce the Twin-Cam to the public in the autumn of 1957, but well before this MG came under pressure not only from their dealers but also from the BMC Competitions Department, to take full advantage of the 1.6-litre International sporting class limit. To do this, it was thought advisable to increase the cylinder bore rather than the crankshaft stroke. The 1,489cc engine's bore was 73.025mm (2.875in), and this was therefore increased to 75.39mm (2.968in). The fact that a 75.68mm cylinder bore would have resulted in a 1,599cc capacity has no relevance here, for BMC's engine builders were still firmly wedded to the idea of using nominal dimensions in Imperial measure—the 1,489cc bore was $2\frac{7}{8}$in, and that of the 1,588cc Twin-Cam was $2\frac{31}{32}$in!

Even though the bore increase was limited to a mere 2.36mm, or 0.093in, it was not possible to achieve this without making changes to the cylinder block casting (which was already, I remind you, considerably different from the push-rod block). Coring changes were made by arranging to 'siamese' the two end pairs of cylinders, thus sacrificing the space between them for water cooling.

An immediate effect of this was that the entire, and very ticklish, question of piston-to-cylinder wall clearances had to be re-assessed and re-developed, as had the profile of the pistons (being finalised for the use of a 9.9:1 compression ratio), along with all the other complications—finalisation of valve timing, ignition timing, oil flow, carburettor settings, for example—which a change of engine capacity inevitably drags along behind it. It might even be suggested that this late change was partly responsible, at least, for the early problems which afflicted the production cars; it certainly delayed the launch of the production car by at least nine months.

By the spring of 1958, however, BMC, and MG, decided that they were indeed ready to take the rather momentous step of offering BMC's (and MG's) first-ever twin overhead camshaft engine to the public. The engineers had done their best, and the sales force were ready to do theirs. Now it all depended on us—the public.

②
Twin-Cam–The Technical Analysis

As I have already made clear in the previous chapter, the MGA Twin-Cam which was finally put on sale in July 1958 was a much more specialised car than it looked. It was also a much more specialised car than the project which BMC's bosses had approved back in 1954/5. At first it had looked easy enough to develop what was really no more than a twin overhead camshaft engine conversion on the basis of the MGA production car, but as work progressed a series of modifications made almost every aspect of the car somewhat different from the pushrod MGA itself. Indeed, between 1958 and 1960, further changes would be made, which would make the Twin-Cam even less like the conventional MGA.

Although the layout of the massively strong chassis frame was exactly the same as that of the pushrod MGA from which it was derived, there were several differences of detail sufficient to make them non-interchangeable. The most notable of these was connected with steering rack position, which had had to be altered to provide clearance from the bulkier twin-overhead camshaft engine. As with the normal MGA, the rack housing was bolted to the front chassis cross-member (and poked out towards each wheel through holes in the front chassis extension); the Twin-Cam engine, though mounted in the same position in the chassis, featured a large and bulky cast-alloy front cover, and this resulted in the fan belt pulley also being further forward, near the base of the radiator. This meant that the rack had to be mounted further forward than on the pushrod cars—about one inch—and although the rack itself is the same, the pinion is different since it is longer than that fitted to the pushrod cars, and allows the same steering column to be retained.

Elsewhere on the chassis frame itself, the changes are minor. To suit the installation of the Dunlop disc brakes, there are different brake pipe/flexible hose mounting brackets, the front engine mounting detail on the right is unique to the Twin-Cam, and there is a different bracket for the mounting of the SU electric fuel pump, towards the rear. Finally, and there is no really vital reason why this should be so, the Twin-Cam chassis frame has a different series of bolt hole spacings across the top of the chassis bulkhead rail ahead of the passenger compartment.

It follows from this description that it was easy enough for a Twin-Cam car to be re-converted back to a pushrod engine specification, especially if the Twin-Cam wheels, brakes and steering were left undisturbed—and this explains why the 1600 De Luxe model appeared so smartly when production of the Twin-Cam itself had ceased. It also explains why some of the surviving cars which originated as Twin-Cams have retrospectively become 'private-enterprise' De Luxes.

Compared with the pushrod MGA, the main front suspension links, the lever-arm shock absorbers (and settings), and the vertical links were all similar, as was the steering rack itself, but the hubs were entirely special, and the steering arms themselves differed from those fitted to the MGA 1500 because they not only had to take account of the new (forward) steering rack position but also had to provide clearance for the brake discs.

The brakes, of course, were Dunlop discs, and were different from any other type of brake ever fitted to MG production sports cars. I have already detailed how the choice of Dunlop brakes was made, and why MG were not able to continue to patronise Lockheed, who supplied the drum brakes for the MGA 1500. The caliper actually used was what I would call the 'standard' Dunlop product of the period, and was supplied, at the same time, to concerns as eminent as Ferrari, Aston Martin (for the DB4), and Jaguar (for the XK150s and for the 3.4-litre/3.8-litre saloons). There was a huge increase in brake rubbed area compared with the MGA 1500 (495sq in for the disc-braked Twin-Cam, 134sq in for the drum-braked MGA 1500), and for this reason it was not necessary to specify a brake servo of any sort. Independent road tests confirmed that the pedal pressures were acceptable, and that retardation was strictly comparable with the MGA 1500. The great advantage, of course, was that the disc-brake installation could be hammered really hard without showing signs of fade, whereas the drum-brake installation of the MGA was by no means as resilient.

(*Above*) For the Earls Court Motor show of 1958, MG showed off a partly sectioned example of the MGA Twin-Cam coupe on a revolving turntable. The rear-wheel disc brakes and rear suspension, the window-winding mechanism, and the detail of body roof construction were all displayed to perfection; (*opposite*) the front half of the same car showed the massive engine, special wheels, Dunlop disc brakes and chassis layout (*both Autocar*)

As with other Dunlop disc-brake installations of the day, the handbrake, operating through a cable linkage, worked on the rear discs by a separate caliper with small pads. This worked well so long as it was kept clean and well lubricated, and so long as the caliper mounted pivots were not allowed to seize up. A badly neglected Twin-Cam handbrake, however, could virtually cease to operate altogether—and this sort of failure tended to occur when the car had been stored for a considerable period.

Although the centre-lock Dunlop wheels were not unique, they were a real rarity. No other true quantity-production car ever specified such wheels, though similar (but light-alloy) wheels were to be found on BRM Grand Prix Cars, and the Jaguar D-Type sports-racing cars, both of which were in use when the Twin-Cam

was being developed. Later, I understand, the limited-production Gordon-Keeble also used such wheels, and these are interchangeable with the Twin-Cam variety. Such wheels, of course, feature peg drive into special hubs, rather than driving through splines.

The tyres specified for the Twin-Cam were 5.90–15in Dunlop RS4 Road Speeds, which we would now look upon as somewhat archaic items, but which were then thought to be a good compromise between the behaviour of a high-speed racing tyre and the comfort and long-life potential of a normal road tyre. The MGA 1500, of course, was fitted with normal 5.60–15in Dunlops, but the uprating had been made necessary by the vastly increased performance of the Twin-Cam, whose maximum speed was about 115mph, compared with perhaps 96–98mph for the pushrod-engined car.

For the original Twin-Cam of 1958, there were virtually no external differences in the body compared with the MGA 1500, and both open Tourer and closed Coupe styles were available. Visually, indeed, from the exterior the only recognition marks were the centre-lock wheels and the discreet little 'Twin-Cam' badges screwed to the bonnet surround panel, immediately behind the air vents from the engine bay, and to the boot lid below the familiar MG octagon badge. It was never obvious, however (and does not seem to have been noted by previous writers about Twin-Cams), that the bonnet panel itself was given a slightly different profile to provide clearance for the rather more bulky Twin-Cam engine. Unlike the MGC, there was no need for a separate and rather obvious bulge to be incorporated into the panel; it was merely given a more obvious curvature from side to side, and was thus slightly humped towards the centre of the car. This bonnet, incidentally, was in light alloy as usual, and when the MGA 1500 was replaced by the MGA 1600 in 1959 (ie, while the Twin-Cam was still in production), the new-style bonnet was commonised across the range.

Inside the cockpit, the instrument panel was almost the same as that of the MGA 1500, except that the speedometer and revcounter were both recalibrated to take account of the higher performance and revving capabilities of the new engine. As something of a 'product planning' feature, the Twin-Cam was also given a leather-covered facia panel. Even with this car, incidentally, you still had to pay extra for the heater and screen washer. A careful comparison between car types shows that the heater in the Twin-Cam was slightly displaced to one side compared with the pushrod-engined cars being built at the same time. Some cars, for sure, were built without a heater, or even without the 'fresh-air kit' option, and have blanking plates on the bulkhead to this day.

There were, incidentally, two types of seats, which sometimes cause confusion. Twin-Cam roadsters, the open variety, were normally supplied with bucket seats identical with those of the MGA 1600, which had asymmetrically styled back rests whose top profile matched the curve of the bodywork immediately behind them, while Coupes had rather larger and more sumptuous seats with squared-up backrests and a padded roll around their cushions to provide more support. One way or another these Coupe seats became known as De Luxe seats, and could also be supplied on open cars; such cars are immediately recognised by the style of the seats themselves, and by the fact that they do not conform to the curve of the body panels behind them. (There were, also, what are known as 'Competition De Luxe' seats, but these were very rare, and were normally only fitted to cars built for racing or rallying.)

A feature of the MGA Twin-Cam was the use of Dunlop disc brakes at front and rear. This is the front suspension and brake installation, which also details the peg-drive location of the centre-lock disc wheels (*BL*)

Hidden away out of sight were further body-shell changes connected with the installation of the bulky new engine. The radiator had had to be moved forward to clear the engine, which resulted in new mountings being needed. New inner wheel arch panels (or engine bay valances, if you prefer an alternative description) were provided to increase space around the carburettor air cleaners and the more expansive exhaust system, while the bulkhead panel had different piercings to suit the modified heater position and the different brake master cylinder arrangements. Nothing, it seemed, was simple and logical at BMC at this time.

The Dunlop disc calipers on the Twin-Cam were mounted behind the line of the back axle, and the handbrake had its own separate mechanical disc-gripping arrangements pivoting to the hydraulic foot-brake caliper itself; this only works well if kept well lubricated and free from corrosion (*BL*)

A description of the engine must come next, because this was the centre of the whole design, indeed the reason for its existence in the first place. By the time the Twin-Cam went on sale, the engine was by no means the simple conversion of the pushrod unit which had originally been intended, but was almost entirely special.

When it was announced, the 1,588cc engine capacity of the MGA Twin-Cam was unique at BMC. Every other B-Series engine in series production had a capacity of 1,489cc, which was the original size introduced with the Morris Oxford/MG Magnette models of the early 1950s. The Twin-Cam's 1,588cc capacity had been reached by specifying a larger cylinder bore, which in turn had necessitated changes to the cylinder block casting, and

The steel-disc centre-lock wheels for the Twin-Cam were provided by Dunlop, and were never used on any other production car, though those fitted to the Gordon-Keeble of the 1960s were of a similar basic design. Dunlop Road Speed tyres were standard on the Twin-Cam; radial-ply Michelin Xs were never offered (*BL*)

this meant that the casting was very different indeed from those being machined for the mass-production 1,489cc cars. Almost all the advantages of mass-production tooling, therefore, had been lost. The *Autocar* technical analysis of 18 July 1958 summarises perfectly what had been done, and how manufacture was carried out:

For ease of production, certain parameters were placed on the design of the cylinder block which, although outwardly resembling the standard B-Series unit, is made from entirely new pattern equipment. Location of main faces from the crankshaft centre line, and main bearing bores are identical. Thus the basic machining can be undertaken on the transfer-matic machines of the production line at the

Austin works at Longbridge (with consequent reduction in costs), and the units are then despatched for finishing at the Morris engine works at Coventry where, in fact, the design and development was undertaken.

So far, so good. Very little common machining could, in fact, take place, for almost everything of the Twin-Cam engine in detail was different. The question of different cylinder block coring, re-positioned cylinder head holding-down studs, and larger cylinder bore have all been mentioned already. There was also the fact that the location of the various auxiliaries had been re-shuffled, that camshaft drive details were entirely special, and that the crankshaft was completely different as well.

The light-alloy cylinder head had gone through several stages of development before being put into production. The road car's engine, therefore, was equipped with what I will call the 'classic' type of twin-cam valve gear, whereby the valves themselves were operated from the cam lobes through the intermediary of inverted bucket tappets, which enclosed the valve springs. This, of course, was the arrangement already adopted for engines as diverse as the Jaguar XK six-cylinder unit, any variety of modern twin-cam Alfa Romeos, and the Coventry-Climax FWA and FPF engines which had already made such an impact on the modern motor racing scene. Nowadays, no self-respecting twin-cam engine would use any other method, and MG were absolutely right to adopt it for themselves. There was one slight oddity which was to have serious implications for the engine's reputation in service; instead of arranging for the bucket tappets to operate inside slim sleeves pressed in to the light-alloy head casting (in the way adopted by Jaguar, for instance), MG's engine had them operating direct in machined barrels in the head casting itself.

Because the valves were large, and equally disposed around the centre line of the cylinders at an included angle of 80 degrees (Jaguar used 70 degrees, by the way), a capacious and almost entirely hemispherical combustion chamber was provided. To achieve the planned maximum output of 68bhp/litre, therefore, it had been necessary to use a very high compression ratio of 9.9:1. Because of the inescapable geometric realities of the hemispherical combustion chamber, this meant that steeply domed pistons had to be specified, and a consequence was that the mixture's initial burning space was effectively crescent-shaped, and with a large

A real bonnetful of engine! The Twin-Cam engine's cylinder head and carburation was a bulky assembly, but there was no installation problem at Abingdon, as the engine was fitted to the rolling chassis before the body shell was dropped on top of it (*Peter Wood*)

surface area. BMC's engineers realised that this made the use of 100-octane fuel almost mandatory, and that strict attention to correct ignition timing would be needed, but they thought that Twin-Cam owners *and* dealers could be persuaded to keep their engines in proper working order.

Front view of the early Twin-Cam production engine, showing that it was at least as wide as it was deep. The distributor drive was located in the new cast front cover (*BL*)

There were short separate inlet manifolds, and two SU H6 carburettors, with $1\frac{3}{4}$in diameter throats, were mounted at a semi-downdraught angle of $22\frac{1}{2}$ degrees. Even though cost limitations meant that cast-iron exhaust manifolds had to be used, their shape was really very efficient; there were two separate castings, one linking cylinders Nos 1 and 4, the other linking 2 and 3, and from the flanges there were separate down pipes, the layout being designed to produce the minimum amount of back pressure and the maximum of extractor effect.

Although the front of the cylinder block itself was much like that of the pushrod engine, it was hidden by a large and complex light-alloy front cover hiding the camshaft drive, the distributor drive, and other details. The camshaft of the pushrod engine was not required to be fitted in the side of the block, but its tunnel was retained, and in that tunnel was a half-speed shaft (or jackshaft), driven from the nose of the crankshaft by single helical gears, and which itself provided a skew gear for driving the oil pump, which was hidden away inside the block on that side of the engine.

The overhead camshafts were then driven by a single, long, Duplex chain originating from that jackshaft. An idler gear was mounted to a pivot on the front cover itself, and there was a chain tensioner also positioned inside the front cover. In laying out the twin-cam cylinder head, the carburettors and inlet manifolds had been positioned on the right side of the unit. Although, as on the pushrod engine, there was still space for the dynamo and the starter motor to be placed on that side, the distributor and its drive had had to be moved; this found a home in the front of the timing case, and was driven by a skew gear from the front of the half-speed shaft.

Not only was this a powerful engine, but it was a powerful-*looking* engine, for there was a big, ribbed, cast-alloy sump, polished light-alloy camshaft covers, and all the attention to detail which goes with a truly exclusive high-performance engine. The fact that it was not only powerful but also rather bulky was a handicap which had to be accepted. When installed in the car, and with the body shell in place, the Twin-Cam appeared to have a 'bonnet-full' of power. This was good for the ego, but bad for the servicing and maintenance aspects, and it was for this reason that two detachable panels were later added to the engine bay valances in the body shell, above and behind the line of the front suspension cross-member.

Behind the engine, there was a specially uprated clutch to look after the increased speed and torque which could be developed by the Twin-Cam engine (its maximum torque was 104lb ft at 4,500rpm, compared with 77lb ft at 3,500rpm for the MGA 1500's pushrod engine, and the Twin-Cam engine produced its maximum power at no less than 6,700rpm). Apart from that, however, the gearbox itself, its wheels, cogs, bearings, and ratios, were all absolutely the same as those used on the normal MGA.

Because of the special hubs needed to accept the rear wheel disc brakes of the Twin-Cam and the peg drive for the centre-lock road wheels, the axle was different, and rather special, compared with the normal B-Series unit fitted to MGA 1500s. The casing had to be special, to pick up on disc brake caliper adaptor mountings, and the half shafts themselves had to be special to match the hubs. The same 4.3:1 crown-wheel-and-pinion ring gear was used, as, at first, was the differential itself, but later in the life of the Twin-

Cam the smaller differential gears also became special, and were never specified on any other type of MGA. (On the MGA 1600 De Luxe—a car which is described in greater detail in the next chapter—the axle was even more strange, because MGA wire-wheel type shafts were used, not Twin-Cam shafts, and they matched the wire-wheel car's differential gearing in the final drive itself.)

At this stage, I should point out that several items of 'competition' equipment were optionally available. MG never offered any engine tune-up items (the engine, in all truth, was really a de-tuned racing engine already, and not very de-tuned, at that), but the close ratio gears which had been used on the 'works' racing and rallying MGAs were on offer, while there was the possibility of a telescopic, adjustable, steering column, a detachable hardtop (with sliding side-screens instead of the flap opening type normally fitted to Twin-Cam tourers), a low competition windscreen, and an optional oil cooler. The oil cooler, in fact, was by no means the same as that optional on pushrod-engined MGAs, but had a different mode of mounting and of positioning in the bodywork at the front of the car. Yet again, it seemed, this was a case where sensible commonisation of parts should have been applied, but where a special kit for the Twin-Cam was developed.

This, then, was the Twin-Cam MGA which was revealed in the summer of 1958, but it soon became clear that the specification had still not entirely been settled, nor was the car completely reliable in every detail. Changes began to be made almost at once, but consideration of these changes, and the points at which they were introduced, truly belongs to the next chapter, when the car's production and service life are described. As it happened, the Twin-Cam would have a production life of just about two years, and the majority of the 2,111 cars built were assembled in the winter of 1958 and the first half of 1959. As far as the MG factory at Abingdon was concerned, it was a short-lived phenomenon, but as far as today's enthusiast is concerned, it is a very special car which will live, in fact and in legend, for many years to come.

Note

When the Twin-Cam engine was announced, it was the only 1,588cc B-Series-derived unit built by BMC, and final assembly, at the Morris Engines Branch factory in Coventry, was on a special production line, at the rate of about five units a day.

From May 1959, however, the MGA 1500 pushrod-engined car gave way to the MGA 1600 which, among other important improvements, was given an enlarged and more powerful pushrod engine of 1,588cc. This, unfortunately, was not part of a wholesale rationalisation of engine capacities by BMC, but merely recognition of the fact that pushrod as well as Twin-Cam MGs had to compete in the 1.6-litre competition class. It was a convenient way, too, of providing the MGA customer with an excuse for changing his car for the 'new model' (the MGA 1500, after all, had been on sale since 1955 without important change), and it resulted in an increased power output of 80bhp (nett) at 5,600rpm.

I should make it clear, even so, that the pushrod 1,588cc engines continued to be machined and assembled at Longbridge, and that no other BMC car was given that capacity. The across-the-range change of size occurred in 1961 when not only the MGA but cars like the Morris Oxfords and 'Farina-styled' MG Magnettes were given 1,622cc engines.

⑧
Twin-Cam in Production
– A Two-year Life

After a great deal of experimental and development work, and late delays caused by the decision to increase the size of its engine from 1,489cc to 1,588cc, the MGA Twin-Cam model finally went into production in the spring of 1958. It took time, however, for engine supplies to build up, and it was not until September that true series production was achieved.

What happened next was a source of great frustration to every enthusiastic MG employee, and has been the cause of discussion— and disappointment—among Twin-Cam devotees ever since. Production built up steadily during the winter of 1958/9, and reached a peak of 313 cars a month in February 1959. Within months, however, it became clear that the demand for Twin-Cams was simply not there, and production of the car was cut back to balance the situation. By October 1959—only fifteen months after the Twin-Cam had been publicly launched—serious production was virtually over. In the last nine months of the Twin-Cam's life, only 90 cars were built, and it was all over by June 1960. In less than two years, only 2,111 Twin-Cams were sold. So what happened, and what should MG and BMC have done to save the day?

There is no point in trying to hide the facts, for every Twin-Cam owner, past and present, knows the story: it was all a question of reliability, and the reputation built up by the car's early problems. The fact that, by the end of 1959, the Twin-Cam was a vastly better, if not quite as fast, car, was neither here nor there. All over the world, it seemed, potential Twin-Cam customers had heard about early cars burning their pistons, greedily consuming oil, and needing constant care and attention to keep them going, and decided not to join such an exclusive club. The fact that the service, development and production engineers had combined to bring

Table 3.1 *MGA Twin-Cam—Month-by-month production figures, 1958–60*

1958	May	4	
	June	31	
	July	3	(Month in which car announced)
	August	12	
	September	109	
	October	116	
	November	98	
	December	135	Total for Year 508
1959	January	148	
	February	313	
	March	261	
	April	216	
	May	208	
	June	172	
	July	79	
	August	24	
	September	92	
	October	7	
	November	14	
	December	16	Total for Year 1,550
1960	January	16	
	February	13	
	March	15	
	April	8	
	May	—	
	June	1	Total for Year 53
			Grand Total 2,111

Note: Each monthly figure represents the number of cars rolling off the *finishing* line at Abingdon.

MGA 1600 De Luxe production began in June 1960—see Table 3.2 (p. 55) for details.

about a transformation, such that the later Twin-Cams were altogether more docile, and completely reformed characters, was not taken into consideration. A very efficient campaign of character assassination, helped along, I'm sure, by jealous rivals whose cars were neither as fast nor as exciting as the Twin-Cam, had been carried out. Only massive expenditure in the form of a re-launch, with stunts carried out to prove the latest model, and with a competition programme to prove the point in the full glare of publicity, would have done the trick. But by this time too much money had already been spent on what was only a limited-production model by BMC's Longbridge standards, and the Twin-Cam was allowed to die.

There was also the question of its price, and the fact that not every Twin-Cam was as fast as it was claimed to be, nor as its specification promised that it *should* be. The clincher, though, was probably the fact that the Big Healey—the definitive Big Healey, that is, the 3000 with the the 2,912cc engine—went on sale in 1959, at a very competitive price, and with a lusty trouble-free performance which made it ideal for development by BMC's Competitions Department. Without the Big Healey, perhaps, the Twin-Cam might not only have become a successful competition car, but might also have had a longer production life.

While researching material for this book, I was lucky enough to be allowed to consult the actual Twin-Cam production records, which are now lodged with BL Heritage Ltd, and which give a fascinating amount of detail about the cars themselves. Extracted from those records is the summary given in Table 3.1 of how production progressed.

At this point, I should review the way in which the various components for the MGA Twin-Cam came together, and should reiterate that almost no actual manufacture ever took place at Abingdon in this period. The pressings for chassis frames came from John Thompson Motor Pressings in the industrial Midlands. The body shells—open Tourers or closed Coupes—were pressed, assembled, and painted at the Morris Bodies Branch in Coventry. The engines were assembled at the Morris Engines Branch in Coventry (which was, incidentally, several miles away from the Bodies Branch). The gearboxes and the rear axles were machined and assembled at BMC transmissions plants in Birmingham. Tyres came from Dunlop in Birmingham, wheels came from Dunlop Rim and Wheel in Coventry, and the Dunlop disc brakes also came from a corner of that Dunlop factory in Coventry, which at this point in history was still the 'Detroit of Britain'.

At Abingdon, the whole rolling chassis was completed before the appropriate body shell was lowered into place, which explains, but does not excuse, the fact that the Twin-Cam went into production with a serious accessibility problem (for mechanics and Do-It-Yourself owners) to almost every item on the engine below cylinder-head level. This problem should have been picked up at the development stage, when engines were no doubt being craned out, and re-assembled, in the experimental department at Abingdon.

When the cars were completed—and in February 1959, on

MG's Abingdon factory in 1958, where the final finish area is crowded with MGA Twin-Cams, Austin-Healey 100-Sixes, and Austin-Healey Sprites, not to mention a large number of pushrod-engined MGAs (*BL*)

average, that meant that 15 new Twin-Cams rolled off the simple assembly lines every working day—they were all taken out on the road for a short shake-down test. That sort of thing could never be tackled by a firm making many thousands of identical 'bread-and-butter' cars, but at MG it was still something of a tradition. The author remembers with pleasure how, as an undergraduate at Oxford, he bicycled the few miles south to see the constant stream of gleaming new MGAs threading their way in and out of the MG factory, all on trade plates, and all clearly being on test.

By the time the Twin-Cam was revealed, on 16 July 1958, its existence had become something of an open secret among the motoring press, and in the industry as a whole. With BMC once again on the crest of a profitable wave, the only surprise was that it should have been delayed for so long. (One reason, for sure, was

41

A Twin-Cam at the start of the body-mounting line at Abingdon—with Big Healey body/chassis units in the gallery above and behind the Twin-Cam chassis (*Peter Wood*)

that in the autumn of 1957 MG's production planners were busily getting ready to build Austin-Healey 100-Six models—final assembly being moved down the road from Longbridge—and that in the spring of 1958 they were getting ready to launch the cheeky and characterful Austin-Healey Sprite, which had been prepared in something of a hurry from a design dreamed up in 1956 by Donald and Geoffrey Healey.)

42

MGA production at Abingdon in 1959/60, with the body of a Twin-Cam just having been lowered on slings to mate with the chassis. Very few Twin-Cams were being built by this stage—all the other cars 'in shot' have pushrod engines (*Peter Wood*)

Although BMC's publicity machine operated in a very efficient manner—not only did the authoritative publications all carry full descriptions and cutaway drawings of the engine in that first week, but *The Autocar* and *The Motor* also published road tests of the car as well—there were very few Twin-Cams to be sold at first. The first four cars were finished in May 1958, the next 31 followed in June, but only three followed in July. When the car was released, therefore, apart from the experimental models under the control of the MG experimental department, there were only about 35 Twin-Cams in existence. (All of which, incidentally, helps to explain why the car's 'works' rallying debut was delayed until the Liège–Rome–Liège rally of August 1958.)

It went on sale at a basic price, in Britain, of £843 for the open Tourer, and £904 for the Coupe, and it is important at this juncture to compare those prices with the British competition. MGA 1500s with pushrod engines were on sale at £663 for the Tourer and £724 for the Coupe, which meant that the Twin-Cam was being sold at a premium of 27 per cent, which was a considerable but (in terms of the performance increase) justifiable difference.

The two-seater Austin-Healey 100-Six (Type BN6), which was newly announced and being assembled at Abingdon when the Twin-Cam was launched, was nominally offered for £817, but that price did not include overdrive and wire wheels. Thus equipped, a BN6 sold for £924, or £1,014 if the optional hardtop was also specified. At first glance, however, a sports car enthusiast was being offered an intriguing choice of cars for a similar amount of money. The Big Healey's top speed was about 111mph, and its standing $\frac{1}{4}$-mile time was 18 seconds; the best of the Twin-Cam tests published showed a top speed of 113mph, and the standing $\frac{1}{4}$-mile sprint in 18 seconds. In Britain the other obvious competition came from the Triumph TR3A. It might not have been as fast in a straight line (its top speed was about 105mph and it took nearly 19 seconds to reach the quarter mile), but it was a rugged and well-proven car, recently updated, splendidly braked since Girling disc brakes had been adopted in 1956/1957—and its basic price was only £699.

The situation was worse in the United States, where it was hoped that the Twin-Cam might find success. The Tourer was priced at $3,345, or $3,495 for the Coupe (a much smaller differential than in the case of the British-market price), while Austin-Healey 100-Six prices started at only $3,087, and it is surely relevant that the elephantine, but rapid, Chevrolet Corvette also sold for $3,631.

MG, therefore, went into the market place with a hefty price tag on the Twin-Cam, one that they thought justified by the very special nature of the specification and all the work which had gone into developing it. The press, as a whole, gave it a generous

The facia and instrument panel of the Twin-Cam—virtually the same as that specified for pushrod-engined MGAs of the period, except that the speedometer and rev counter have been recalibrated. On this pre-production car, the rev-counter is 'yellow-lined' at 6,500rpm, and 'red-lined' at 7,000rpm (*BL*)

welcome, and brief comments from those two paragons of motoring journalism, *Autocar* and *Motor*, serve to illustrate how it was received.

The Autocar's technical analysis suggested that: 'The price to be paid for the extra performance and increased braking is not unreasonable, and this latest product from Abingdon must rank among the world's outstanding sports cars ...', while in their road test they commented that: '... The car is quite happy at 100mph for long stretches on Continental roads'. However, one cautionary note was struck, which must surely have chilled the hearts of MG development engineers:

All maximum speed and acceleration tests were carried out with 100 octane petrol. With this, and Belgium premium petrol (89 research octane rating), the engine tended to 'run on' after being switched off. It also used a considerable amount of oil; five pints were added to the sump during one journey of 800 miles, and an overall oil consumption figure of 1,020mpg was recorded.

Motor, like *Autocar*, mentioned in their road test that the Twin-Cam was a relatively noisy beast, particularly in terms of mechanical clamour from the engine bay. On the other hand, they went overboard about their car's performance (which was, in fact, considerably more impressive than that supplied to *Autocar*—see Appendix E (p. 216) for further details): '... of all the cars so far tested by *Motor* only machines built specifically for sports-car racing would keep pace with this 1,600cc touring two-seater in a standing start match to speeds of 60, 70 or 80mph.' Unhappily, they also discovered that they could make the engine 'pink' on German 97-octane fuel, that it 'ran-on' when switched off, no matter what fuel was being used, and that it consumed one pint of oil every 120 miles, which equates almost exactly to *Autocar*'s experiences.

Clearly no accusations of bias, or partiality, could be levelled at either team of testers, for with different cars (PMO 326 for *Autocar*, PMO 325 for *Motor*, both being Tourers) they recorded the same subjective impressions. Both teams, incidentally, loved the handling, enthused over the brakes, and enjoyed the ambience of this type of sports car motoring.

They had, however, put their collective fingers on the major service problem which soon faced MG. Almost every early Twin-Cam, whether used in Britain, in North America, or in Europe, seemed to suffer from an acute sensitivity to ignition timing and to the type of fuel being used, and all of them seemed to consume a great deal of engine oil. It was not long, indeed, before the first reports of piston burning began to filter back to the factory and, since the behaviour of these cars was closely watched by other enthusiasts all over the world, the word soon got around that the Twin-Cam's engine was not to be trusted.

The story of the Twin-Cam over the next eighteen months, therefore, is the story of the fight to sort out the behaviour of the engine, a fight which was eventually won by the development engineers, but one which went on too long to allow the car to survive. Thus, even before I describe the events, and the other modifications in the short career of the Twin-Cam, I must detail

The very neat exterior handle detail of the MGA Coupe's doors. The same feature was, of course, used on Twin-Cam coupes. Tourers never had exterior handles of any type (*BL*)

the engine problems, and the modifications made.

First there was the problem of the oil consumption, which was not directly responsible for any of the engine failures (not, that is, if the Twin-Cam owner checked his dipstick at every fuel halt, when he usually found that he had to pour two pints into the engine for every 10 gallons of fuel bought). Intrinsically, this was caused by the rush to develop the piston and ring profiles to suit the enlarged (1,588cc) engine, which had only been decided upon at a late stage in the evolution of the model. It is by no means easy to arrive at an acceptable compromise between cylinder bore wear, piston ring-to-cylinder wall friction, and piston shape even when development can be taken at a measured pace.

The original engines had oil scraper piston rings without expanders, and the eventual solution was to substitute a new ring giving more adequate sealing qualities; these rings had expanders inside, and were fitted from Engine No 16GB/U/2057 to the end of Twin-Cam production. This change, incidentally, took place in cars assembled from May 1959. Even so, the new rings (which carry BMC Part No AEH 672) did not cure the problem completely, and it was a lucky Twin-Cam owner who ever drove his car quickly and recorded better than 2,000mpg of oil.

Sorting out the pre-ignition problem—for this is what it was— took time, and several distinctly different changes. The fact was that the original Twin-Cam engine was extremely sensitive to ignition timing and to the quality of fuel used. All Twin-Cam engines should really have been treated to a diet of 100-plus-octane fuel, which was available in Britain and the United States, but not available at all in Europe and most parts of the world.

The initial combination of Champion N5 plugs, over-advanced ignition, lower-grade fuel and a 'top-limit' compression ratio—or even not all of these items—could soon result in pre-ignition or 'pinking', and sometimes even in the piston crowns being holed, with disastrous consequences. The short-term answer was to change the grade of plug (from N5 to N3—interestingly enough, *Motor*'s test car of July 1958 *had* N3s), to make sure that the static ignition setting was always Top Dead Centre and not a degree earlier, and also to plead with the owner to use the best possible grade of fuel. A Service Bulletin, dated 21 April 1959 (which appeared far too late—it was almost a case of bolting the stable door after the horse had gone) recommended the use of N3 sparking plugs 'which give better heat conditions at the piston crown', and assured dealers that warranty claims would be accepted in respect of this change—which presumably included the rebuilding of the engines with new pistons!

Months after that (it was actually notified on 31 December 1959, by which time series production of the Twin-Cam was over) BMC Service Ltd issued a terse little pamphlet entitled 'Getting the Best from your MGA Twin-Cam', whose front page was placarded with PLEASE READ BEFORE DRIVING. This rather laboured the points already made earlier in this chapter, and made the point that '...fuels with an octane rating below 93 are **not** suitable', and that: 'It is recommended that fuel with an octane rating between 95 and 98 be used under normal touring conditions but when optimum performance is required the use of fuel rated between 99 and 101 octane will be found beneficial.' Later they mentioned the sparking plug story, the choice of N58R plugs for competition work, and the need for accurate ignition setting. In bold print, in the last words of the pamphlet, they insisted that **'Under no circumstances should the ignition be advanced beyond TDC.'**

While all this was going on, several different piston crown shapes were being tried (the Twin-Cam Parts Book is accurate, and comprehensive, on this point), but in the end BMC engineers had to bow to the inevitable truth—that the compression ratio had always been too high and the combustion space by no means ideal, and that the ratio would have to be reduced. For Engine No 2251 (fitted to a Twin-Cam built in June 1959) and all subsequent engines, a reduced compression ratio piston was specified. The new ratio was 8.3:1—just the same as that of the pushrod-engined MGAs, incidentally—and it allowed normal premium, as opposed to super premium, fuels to be used. Many engines were subsequently rebuilt using these low-compression pistons, which resulted in a drop in maximum power, from 108bhp to 100bhp, and in a dramatic improvement in reliability.

There was one other engine problem which should be mentioned—a problem which has almost certainly been eradicated on all surviving units. Almost as soon as the car had gone out on sale, it was discovered that there were circumstances where the inverted bucket tappets surrounding the valves in the cylinder head could slightly tilt, jam, and cause destruction of the valve gear. This was because they were too short, so from Engine No 1087 (ie, after 586 engines had been built) the tappets were lengthened from 1.25 to 1.50in. Finally to sort out the valve gear, from Engine No 1587—after a further 500 engines had been built—slim steel sleeves were inserted into the cylinder head so that the tappets could work up and down without tending to 'pick-up' in the aluminium head casting itself.

Now to the good news, for, apart from the well-publicised

Many Twin-Cams, such as this 1959/60 model (sporting MGA 1600 styling features) found their way to North America. This car carries a Maryland registration plate and has modern-style Michelin radial-ply tyres (*Peter Wood*)

engine problems, the Twin-Cam led a robust and reliable life. Changes made to the chassis, and to the bodywork, were only introduced to make it easier to work on, or to bring it in line with changes being made to pushrod-engined MGAs. As I have already mentioned, early operating experience with Twin-Cams had shown that access to things like the dynamo and starter, the oil filter, the distributor, and other accessories hidden from view under the massive twin-cam head and carburettors, was poor. Therefore, from Chassis No 592 (ie, after only 91 production cars had been built, in September 1958), body shells began to be fitted with two louvred access panels which followed the same profile as the inner wheel arches, or engine bay valances, but which could be unscrewed and put to one side. These were positioned above and behind the line of the front suspension cross-member, and improved the servicing aspect considerably. As they were not needed on pushrod-engined cars, they were never standardised on the other models.

The only chassis specification change of any note came at Chassis No 2275 (for cars built from June 1959), when the front anti-roll bar which had been optional for competition purposes became standard equipment. This, however, was not a minor change, for it also entailed a new front chassis extension (the pressing which bolted up to the front cross-member) to mount the bar, and new lower wishbones were also needed for the bar's links to connect up to the suspension linkage. At the same time, incidentally, this modification became optional (though not standard) on the pushrod-engined MGAs.

The Twin-Cam models received one significant visual change, when the new front and rear lamp details for the MGA 1600 were phased in for the Twin-Cam as well. These involved a new yellow and white side lamp/flashing indicator assembly at the front, and a new lighting plinth at the rear incorporating a separate indicator lamp above a combined stop/tail lamp unit. Introduction points were Chassis No 2193 (Tourer) and 2292 (Coupe), the change taking place in June 1959.

And now, briefly, to the important cars, and the important junctures, in the two-year life of the MGA Twin-Cam. The identity of the Twin-Cam prototypes is not known to me, but it seems from the production records held by BL Heritage that, although there were no pre-production 'proving cars' as such, the first few 'production cars' were used for just that purpose. The very first production Twin-Cam carried Chassis No 501, and started down the assembly lines on 22 April 1958. (MG, no doubt, would have liked it to have the number of 251, which used to be a traditional 'first number' at Abingdon, because it was MG's telephone number, but all such sentimental nonsense had been stopped by BMC when the MG TF was announced in 1953. On the other hand, why should it have been 501? No-one now remembers ...) No 501 was not the first Twin-Cam to be completed, however, for four other cars were finished in May, whereas 501 was not ready for delivery until the first week of June. 501 and 502, incidentally, were both destined for use as demonstration cars, although they were not actually registered for road use until the end of July.

The first 50 Twin-Cams were all Tourers, this number including all the cars to be used for test by the press, other demonstration cars, two cars (one red, one green) for the Competitions Department, and examples for delivery to British racing enthusiasts like

One identification point which pinpoints a late-model, 1959/60, Twin-Cam is the tail-lamp cluster, which was brought into line with the cluster specified for pushrod-engined MGA 1600s in the summer of 1959 (*BL*)

Colin Shove (525), Geoff Dear (526) and Ted Lund (527).

The first batch of Coupes started with Chassis No 551, which was finished on 16 September 1958, and went to Geoff Holt. A few days later 573 (a Tourer) went to Dick Jacobs, 596 (a Coupe) was delivered to Competitions, and 652 (a Tourer) was delivered to John Gott, who was not only BMC's rallying team captain, but was also the Chief Constable of Northamptonshire.

After the Earls Court Motor Show of October 1958, when a partly sectioned sandy gold Twin-Cam Coupe was put on display on a revolving turntable, production began to swing more purposefully into gear. 98 cars were finished off in November, and 135 in December, but no less than 148 followed in January 1959, and an astonishing 313 in February—the best-ever monthly figure, in the shortest month of the year! True series production of 1959-calendar-year models began soon after Chassis No 1000, for 508 cars were completed during 1958. In the week before Christmas, incidentally, a quartet of Coupes had been allocated to the Competitions Department, and these were eventually prepared for racing at Sebring in March 1959.

The rush of Twin-Cam production in the early months of 1959 is obvious from Table 3.1 above, and from these facts:

Ch No 1000 was finished on 31 December 1958
Ch No 1500 followed on 27 February 1959
Ch No 2000 was completed on 29 April 1959.

But by this time the Twin-Cam was well over its peak, due to the rapid erosion of its reputation by the engine problems experienced on earlier cars. In July 1959, for the first time in ten months, Twin-Cam production at Abingdon plunged below 100 cars a month, and it never recovered. After a brief resurgence in September, October production dropped like a stone to a mere seven cars, and the life of the Twin-Cam was effectively over.

The first 1960-calendar-year car to be completed carried the Chassis No 2558. On 16 February 1960 five British Racing Green Tourers—2571 to 2575 inclusive—were delivered to the Competitions Department, for speedy preparation as Sebring 12-hour race cars, and on 13 April the last series-production car of all, 2610, a Tourer, rolled off the production line.

An astonishing thing then happened. Mike Ellman-Brown, an MG enthusiast through and through, got to know that the Twin-Cam was to be discontinued, determined to have the last one of all, and badgered John Thornley for it. 2610, however, had already left the factory, and in the end Thornley agreed that one further example should be built. Six weeks later, therefore, Chassis No 2611, a Tourer (noted as: Reference Mr J. W. Thornley in the production records) made its way down the tracks among a flood of MGA 1600s, was completed on 3 June 1960, and was collected there and then by its doting owner. Ellman-Brown was as faithful to his new car as he had been to its reputation for, more than twenty years later, he still owns that car.

In some ways, however, the spirit of the Twin-Cam refused to die, for in the next two years a very shadowy and somewhat mysterious model—the 1600 De Luxe—came to be produced.

How and why this car, with its roots in the Twin-Cam layout, came into existence is now related in the following note.

Note: The MGA 1600 De Luxe—a mystery solved at last

Previous books about MG cars have acknowledged the existence of an MGA 1600 De Luxe model, but have not been able to pinpoint all the details of its life, or how many of each type were built. The mystery is now solved. A truly painstaking look through the MGA production records, now preserved for all time by BL Heritage, has allowed me to identify the De Luxes, how many were made, when, and in what condition. The details follow.

There has never been any mystery about the origins of the model. After the last MGA Twin-Cam was built in the late spring of 1960, MG found themselves with stocks, or unbreakable forward commitments, of Twin-Cam chassis frames and all the special suspensions, steering, brakes and road wheels appropriate to that car. Accordingly, they decided to market, on a very low-key basis, a car which they called De Luxe, which effectively used these Twin-Cam parts but was powered by the perfectly standard 1600 pushrod overhead valve engine of the day. As with other MGAs, the De Luxe was available in open Tourer or as a closed Coupe.

The very first De Luxe was Chassis No 91240. It began its journey down the chassis line on 28 April 1960—in other words, *after* series production of Twin-Cams had ended, but *before* work began on the final Twin-Cam which Mike Ellman-Brown bought in June 1960. In fact, the completion of that first production-line De Luxe was delayed until 9 June 1960, which was, neatly and tidily, *after* the very last Twin-Cam had been driven out of the building. That first car was identified in the production records as a Demonstrator, in Home Market condition, after which series production (in limited numbers) got under way. The last De Luxe of all was Chassis No 108652, and was finished off on 1 June 1962, just a week before MGA production finished altogether.

I ought to make it clear that not all De Luxes were built to the same Twin-Cam chassis specification, and not all had the same number of optional extras fitted to the early De Luxe models at least. Indeed, by the spring of 1962, it is clear from the production records that the production planners at Abingdon were trying very hard to use up whatever stocks of parts they retained, before MGA production was finally stopped altogether. A look at the statistical evidence shows that 164 so-called De Luxes were built in the last ten weeks of MGA production—a massive 42 per cent of all De Luxe production—which was certainly not occasioned by a last-minute upsurge in demand for the cars.

This is how production of De Luxes progressed:

Table 3.2   *MGA 1600 De Luxe production—1960 to 1962*

—at first with 1,588cc engine		Tourer	Coupe
1960	June	16	1
	July	7	—
	August	6	—
	September	2	1
	October	4	—
	November	15	1
	December	—	1
1961	January	3	3
	February	3	2
	March	12	3
	April	2	—

—changeover then made to 1,622cc engine, and Mk II style and detail specification.

		Tourer	Coupe
	June	2	—
	July	33	1
	August	34	1
	September	16	—
	October	7	7
	November	18	2
	December	6	1
1962	January	7	3
	February	2	6
	March	1	2
	April	86	—
	May	66	—
	June	12	—
Totals	1600 De Luxe	70	12	82 in all
	1600 Mk II De Luxe	290	23	313 in all
Grand Total		360	35	395 in all

I should also make it clear that a true De Luxe should not have had the special Twin-Cam body shell details (such as the extra engine bay access panels in the valences), but should have been based on the normal MGA 1600 or MGA 1600 Mk II shell. Mechanically, a De Luxe should have had the Twin-Cam chassis, suspension, brakes, steering and wheels, but it had the normal pushrod engine and gearbox appropriate to the 1600 or 1600 Mk II model of the day. Detail of the hybrid back-axle specification has already been mentioned in Chapter 2.

An MG Service Bulletin, dated 30 August 1960, states that: 'Disc brakes (front and rear) and centre lock wheels are now made available as optional extras. Steering assembly, front suspension and rear axle are modified to suit.' This makes it quite clear that the De Luxe was never really meant to be a regularly advertised extra model, and it explains why I have not been able to trace a price, in the UK or in North America, for such cars.

Observant statisticians will already have added the total of 395 De Luxes to 2,111 Twin-Cams, and come up with the figure of 2,506. Apart from the fact that this includes five cars built in Competitions, I am convinced that this means that the *original* Twin-Cam 'sanction' (a motor industry term for the number of components ordered for production of a particular car) was 2,500, and that this was a tidy way of getting rid of parts already ordered or even delivered when Twin-Cam production ended.

It is interesting to note that there were so very few Coupes—only 12 1600s, and 23 1600 Mk IIs—and it is also interesting to note that there were many more Mk IIs than ordinary 1600s. The probable reason for this, however, has already been explained.

Seven of the 35 Coupes were 'works' competition cars. Chassis Numbers 104428 and 104429 were delivered to the Competitions Department in October 1961, but only one of them, 104429, was actually used as a rally car, and was the famous 1962 Coupe, registered 151 ABL. Three other cars—Chassis Numbers 106073, 106074 and 106075—were actually built up in the Competitions Department, rather than along the production lines, and were the 1962 Sebring race cars. The two 1961 De Luxe Coupes were not noted in MG chassis records as De Luxes, but it is significant that 100148 and 100149 were for Sebring, and were built in March 1961.

The production records show not only that the De Luxes were given whatever chassis numbers were conveniently available at the time (the only way that they could be identified in the records was that the details of their body and trim colours were written down in a different colour of ball point pen by the records clerk), but that most of them were loaded up with other extras such as special seats, close ratio gearboxes, different axle ratios, and oil coolers.

How many of the *true* De Luxes now survive?

④
Twin-Cams in Motor Sport

It would not be practical for me to summarise the competition record of every twin-cam engined car built by MG in the 1950s and 1960s—space simply does not allow this—but MG's own factory involvement in record-breaking, racing and rallying was very significant, and deserves study. I have already shown, in Chapter 1, the way in which the twin overhead camshaft MG engine evolved, and was developed. Now it is time to detail the way in which the unit figured in record-breaking and racing expeditions even before it was put on sale to the public.

Normally, when a radically new design is being developed, the British motor industry finds it difficult to hold the secret, and leaks like a sieve. Somehow, in the case of the BMC twin-cam engine developments, this did not happen. Therefore, when not one, but two, engines were revealed for use in the prototype EX182 MGAs in the Tourist Trophy race of September 1955, it was a real surprise, not only for the general public, but for MG's competitors as well. Indeed, there is evidence to suggest that Standard-Triumph's intention to design a twin overhead camshaft engine for use in Triumph TRs effectively stems from that time.

To summarise, MG had built four prototype MGAs earlier in 1955, with light-alloy bodies and with special cross-flow Weslake cylinder heads for their B-Series pushrod engines. Three cars raced at Le Mans in June 1955. Two finished strongly—in twelfth and seventeenth places. One, unhappily, was wrecked in a high-speed accident at White House corner, and its driver, Dick Jacobs, was grievously injured. For the Tourist Trophy race in Northern Ireland, around the Dundrod road circuit, three cars were entered, one was more or less equipped to road-car standards and used the Le Mans type of pushrod overhead valve engine, the two others, with full lightweight bodies and other modifications, were fitted with twin overhead camshaft engines, one of the Gerald Palmer/

Morris Engines design, the other of the Appleby/Longbridge design. The Morris-engined car was also fitted with Girling front-wheel disc brakes and was given reprofiled front wings, in which the much smaller 'headlamps' were mounted very low down. Those lamps, incidentally, would never have been pronounced legal by British authorities, as they were much too close to the ground. In any case, they were too small to be effective—in fact they were the auxiliary lamps normally fitted to the Riley Pathfinder saloons currently being assembled at Abingdon! The Austin-engined car, on the other hand, looked much more like the MGA production car, announced the following week, except that it had a rather angular bonnet bulge to provide clearance over the top of the special Austin engine.

It is here, incidentally, that the futility of always identifying a competition car by its registration number becomes apparent. The Morris-engined TT twin-cam was pictured, at Abingdon, as LBL 301; on the other hand, the car which had been totally and absolutely wrecked at Le Mans had also carried the number LBL 301 before the 24-hour race! One other source has suggested that the TT car was actually LBL 304, 'which had finished twelfth at Le Mans', though I have always understood that this was the spare car for Le Mans, and that it was LBL 302 which took twelfth place. In any case—and therefore how are we to prove *anything*?— the Le Mans and TT cars actually raced without numbers of any description!

The fate of the Austin twin-cam engine is easily related. Pre-race testing showed that it produced very little more power than the Le Mans pushrod B-Series engine, because its rev limit was the same. Marcus Chambers also told me that there were problems with the twin-choke Solex carburettors. The engine, therefore, was removed before the car actually left for Northern Ireland, and a Le Mans-type pushrod engine was fitted in its place.

The Morris-designed twin-cam showed much more promise, and it was the late decision to fit Weber carburettors instead of Solex which probably sealed its fate. To make the swap, special fabricated inlet manifolds were needed, but their welded joints had hair-line cracks which expanded as the engine got hot, let in air downstream of the carburettors themselves, weakened the mixture, and caused misfiring. (This problem, in fact, was only identified *after* the car returned to Abingdon.) The result was that

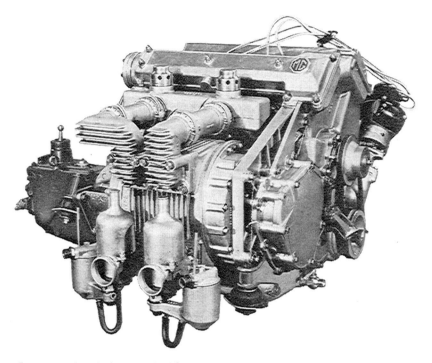

In 1957 and again in 1959, BMC sent the mid-engined MG EX181 record car to the Bonneville Salt Flats in Utah, USA, to establish straight-line speeds of 245 and 254mph respectively. In each case the engine used was a mightily supercharged derivative of the Twin-Cam engine, the 'blower' being supplied by Shorrock (*BL*)

although the new engine produced more power, and gave the car more performance, than the pushrod engine used in the other two machines, it did not last, and had to be retired after 34 laps of the 84-lap, seven-hour race.

The Austin-design twin-cam engine was never seen again, and it is thought that no further development was carried out. The Morris-designed unit, which henceforth I will now call the Twin-Cam engine, also went into hiding for a time, but periodically reappeared in record cars built by MG at Abingdon.

In August 1956, the 1954 record car, EX179, was sent to the Bonneville Salt Flats in Utah, USA, to attack sprint and endurance targets. EX179, incidentally, was based on the chassis frame and suspensions of the prototype EX175 (or MGA project) of 1952, in fact this being the second prototype frame which Syd Enever had

had built. For EX179, it was liberally drilled. The shape of EX179 was very similar to that of the famous (1938-vintage) reincarnation of EX135, though the two shells were quite different in size and detail. In 1954 form, EX179 had had a TF-type of engine, and was left-hand-drive. For 1956, and with the need to channel the prototype Twin-Cam engine's exhaust gases out of the bonnet on the left side of the car, it was converted to right-hand-drive, which effectively meant that the driving seat, steering wheel and pedals swapped sides with the big fuel tank (which occupied the 'passenger seat'), and the driver's headrest was re-arranged to suit.

Two different prototype Twin-Cam engines were used, one in 'sprint' and one in 'endurance' tune—the 'sprint' engine having no less than 120bhp. Camshaft and piston profiles were obviously still at the experimental stage, but both engines were of 1,489cc, both were unsupercharged, and both used normal high-octane pump fuel. Since, by this time, the MGA production car was already on the market and selling well, particularly in North America, BMC publicity staff thought they could reasonably stretch the truth a bit. For this purpose, EX179 was described as a modified MGA, having a special version of the B-Series engine, and a streamlined body!

With the 'sprint' engine installed, EX179 took the International Class F Flying 10-mile record at 170.15mph, which was 16mph better than was achieved with the TF-engined EX179 in 1954, and only 6.5mph slower than the old EX135 record car had achieved, post war, in 1948 when fitted with a prototype *two-litre* Jaguar engine. The Twin-Cam engine, clearly, had deep-breathing lungs already. All that was really necessary was to prove its endurance.

In 1956 this proved to be more difficult, but it was no fault of the engine. First time out, the 'endurance' car ran for $5\frac{1}{4}$ hours before a rear hub bearing failed. Second time out, however, on 15 August, there was no mistake, and EX179 blared its way consistently around the circular 10-mile course for more than twelve hours, taking a total of 16 International Class F (1,500cc) records; the twelve hours were completed at 140.71mph. Taking American National records into consideration, the Twin-Cam engined EX179 came away with no fewer than 64 new record marks to its credit.

No other endurance records were ever attempted, or achieved, by a Twin-Cam engined car. In 1957 and 1959, on the other hand, MG produced a far more exciting record car. There was no question of this one ever being called a modified MGA by BMC staff, as it was almost entirely special from end to end. Apart from the use of a much modified Twin-Cam engine, it had a tubular chassis frame, the engine was mounted behind the driver, and it had the most remarkable aerodynamic profile ever to be seen on a special MG.

By any standards—and even by the standards of the 1980s, which is getting on for a quarter of a century after it was designed—the new car, coded EX181, was a phenomenal design. Conceived in 1956 by Syd Enever, and designed for him by Terry Mitchell of the MG design staff, EX181 used a mid-engined layout at a time when no post-war manufacturer of racing cars except for John Cooper had done the same. It also exhibited what has since been known as a 'tear-drop' shape which made no concessions whatsoever to the components to be packed into it, and it must have been one of the very first competition cars ever laid down where the shape of the body came first, and took priority over all else. There was a superficial resemblance (but it *was* only superficial) to John Cobb's Railton Special Land Speed Record Car, which is to say that the car was at its widest near the nose, and that there was a long and tapering tail. Indeed, it was this shape, allied to its tiny size, which more or less determined the mechanical layout, with the central driving position up front, and the engine located behind him.

The Twin-Cam engine was central, not only in the design, but *to* the design. The main frame was based on two large-diameter longitudinal tubes, with MGA-type independent front suspension and rack and pinion steering, while there was De Dion rear suspension, with springing by splayed-out quarter-elliptic cantilever leaf springs, and further fore-and-aft location by radius arms. The wheelbase was 8ft 0in, the overall length including a very long tail was 15ft 1.5in, while the overall height was a mere 2ft 6in to the top of the main shell and 3ft 2.25in to the top of the cowl over the driver's helmet. The most remarkable statistic of all concerned the drag coefficient, which was quoted as $K = 0.000292$ (as near to perfect as could be arranged if a vehicle has to have wheels on the ground), and which required a mere 145bhp to reach 200mph. The flat-out target of this sprint car, however, was four miles a

The team captain calculates his time schedule! John Gott, who drove this Twin-Cam coupe, RMO 101, on the 1959 Monte Carlo Rally, waits time at a control in France. The equipment on this 'works' rally car includes Dunlop Weathermaster tyres and snow mats (*Autocar*)

minute, or 240mph, at which speed it was calculated that 240bhp would be required. To accelerate the car up to this speed, a conventional four-speed synchromesh gearbox was mounted in unit with the engine (but not the normal B-Series box—in essence it was a Riley RMA box), and the special spiral bevel final drive had alternative ratios of 1.94:1 or 1.825:1. Very special small-diameter Dunlop tyres were needed, on conventional five-stud fixing 15in road wheels.

The engine itself, which may have started life as an experimental Twin-Cam unit, was very special indeed. True, it was still of 1,489cc, and used the basic Twin-Cam cylinder head and breathing arrangements, but it had a specially stiffened cylinder block (the ribs are obvious in pictures of the unit), a compression ratio of 6.75:1, and a huge supercharging installation developed for MG by Chris Shorrock around a commercial vehicle unit he had already designed. This eccentric vane supercharger was gear-driven from the nose of the enlarged and stiffened crankshaft, drew its intake air through two SU carburettors with $2\frac{3}{16}$in throats, and pushed mixture into the cylinders at a maximum pressure of 2.2 atmospheres, or 32 psi. In his *Autocar* analysis of the project, Harry Mundy made the point that the 1955 and 1956 Twin-Cams had used valve gear rather like the designs used in Wolseley 6/80 and 6/90 engines of the late 1940s and early 1950s (which is to say that inverted tappets were screwed into the large-diameter hollow valve stems), but that this special record engine had bucket tappets sliding up and down inside sleeves cast integral with the valve guides. (Even this, be it noted, was not the final layout of production Twin-Cams, whose tappets slid up and down in direct contact with the light-alloy cylinder heads at first, or inside thin-wall sleeves after a certain point.)

Although the maximum power output target had been 280bhp, this was exceeded in testing at Coventry. The engine installed in EX181 produced no less than 290bhp at 7,300rpm, with a remarkable maximum torque figure of 216lb ft at 5,600rpm, and the back-up engine was reputed to be even slightly stronger than that!

Stirling Moss had been contracted to drive EX181 at the Bonneville Salt Flats, immediately after he had driven the Vanwall in the Pescara Grand Prix in Italy (a race which, incidentally, he won—the Vanwall's first World Championship success outside Great Britain), and the driving compartment had been tailored around his rather short frame. The American Phil Hill did all the pre-attempt testing, which included assessing the possibilities of 36.2mph/1,000rpm or 38.6mph/1,000rpm gearing. As it happens, Hill achieved the necessary target speeds before Moss arrived from Europe (though it was decided not to claim these figures, as the publicity machine was all angled towards the combination of Moss and MG), and the 36.2mph/1,000rpm gearing was used, with which the much-boosted Twin-Cam engine was turning over at about 6,800rpm, some 500rpm below its peak.

Things were nearly ruined on 17 August, when heavy rain flooded the marked straight track on the Salt Flats, and since the course had only been booked for a further week (and since, in any case, Stirling Moss would shortly have to leave for another racing engagement) it looked at one time as if the attempt would have to be abandoned. By Friday, 23 August, however, the track had dried

John Gott, navigated by Ray Brookes, urging his 'works' Twin-Cam coupe around a corner close to the Col de Braus where his rally came to a premature end in the 1959 Monte (*Autocar*)

out sufficiently, Moss duly took EX181 out for the attempt, and set up five new International Class F (1,500cc) sprint records, the best speed being the Flying kilometre at no less than 245.64mph.

Even so, MG thought they could not only go faster, but pick up some different records as well. No record attempts were made in 1958 (the whole of the MG workforce at Abingdon were occupied in getting the MGA Twin-Cam, the Austin-Healey Sprite, and further derivations of the Big Healey into production), but in 1959 the same team returned to Utah for another go. This time the supercharged Twin-Cam engine had been enlarged to 1,506cc— by the simple expedient of boring out by 0.015in, to a new (metric) dimension of 73.426mm cylinder bore—and the target was Class E (2,000cc maximum) records. It will be recalled that MG did this on a previous occasion—in 1939, when Major 'Goldie' Gardner's EX135 was over-bored, quite literally overnight, so that it could tackle 1,500cc targets soon after setting up new 1,100cc speeds on a German autobahn.

1600 'De Luxe' models were rare, and were really Twin-Cams with pushrod MGA engines fitted. These two cars were 1,588cc De Luxe Coupes raced at Sebring in 1961, having been prepared by the Competitions Department at Abingdon. They took first and second places in their capacity class (*BL*)

The engine's power output had been increased slightly, to 303bhp at 7,300rpm, but a more significant improvement was to EX181's already excellent aerodynamics. The vertical stabilising fins, so strongly recommended by Captain George Eyston, were removed, and it was found in the Armstrong-Whitworth wind tunnel that a reduction of seven per cent in the drag had been achieved. On this occasion Stirling Moss was not available, so Phil Hill drove the car, and set up six new Class E records—the fastest being the Flying kilometre, at 254.91mph. The existing records, incidentally, had been held by EX135, and had been set up in 1951, when the ageing but very versatile car had been fitted with a special 2-litre version of the six-cylinder Wolseley 6/80's engine.

It was after this, with EX181 clearly at its limit, that John Thornley was no longer able to justify the chasing of more and yet more records, most of which were held by an MG car in any case. EX181's 254.91mph, therefore, was the last, and the most phenomenal, of all the MG records set up between 1930 and 1959. No further MG record attempts have ever been made.

In the meantime, of course, there had been changes in corporate policy regarding BMC cars and competitions activity. By the time the MGA Twin-Cam production car was put on sale, in the summer of 1958, the BMC Competitions Department had been given the job of making BMC a world-class contender in rallying, without restriction on the type of cars they could choose. Accordingly, the 'Big Healey' became available to them for the very first time.

This could not have happened at a worse time for the Twin-Cam, which also became available for rallying use just a few months later. While the Twin-Cam was still at the prototype stage, the Competitions Department was struggling to achieve credibility, and was mainly using pushrod-engined MGAs. There had always been the promise of homologated quantity-production Twin-Cams, first before the end of 1957, and then before summer 1958, but the sudden availability of the 'Big Healey' almost sealed the fate of the Twin-Cam, even before it had properly been committed to a development programme. Even though it was only fitted with a very ordinary pushrod six-cylinder engine, the Big Healey had so much more potential.

In his autobiography, *Seven Year Twitch*, published in 1962, Marcus Chambers, who was BMC's Competitions Manager from

The Lund-Escott 'private' Twin-Cam at Le Mans in 1959, immediately after it had collided with a dog at high speed, and immediately before the transmission seized owing to overheating. The damage done to the grille and the undertray in the accident is obvious (*Autocar*)

1955 to 1962, said: 'We had, at one time, hoped to enter five twin-cam MGAs [for the 1958 Alpine Rally], but for a number of reasons this was not possible and at the last minute we decided to enter the same number of Austin-Healey 100-Sixes.' The 'number of reasons' included the fact that the Alpine Rally started on 7 July, whereas the Twin-Cam's public launch was eventually delayed until 16 July, so it could not possibly be used, for homologation for sporting purposes was needed, and there was no 'prototype' class on this particular event.

'Comps', however, lost no time in taking delivery of Twin-Cams for future use. The records show that cars numbered 524 (a green Tourer), 528 (a red Tourer), and 596 (a red Coupe) all went 'across the yard' to the department in the first few months. 524 was delivered in June 1958, before the Twin-Cam was officially announced, but it was 528, delivered in August, which was the first Twin-Cam to appear in an event. Registered as PRX 707, and given a detachable black hardtop, it was entrusted to John Gott and Ray Brookes for the gruelling Liège-Rome-Liège Rally.

There had been very little time to prepare the car for the event— Marcus Chambers' book tells us that it was standard apart from a 20-gallon fuel tank, special seats, extra lamps and instruments, under-shielding and a few other details—so it could not be expected to dispute the top few places. As it happened, the car finished ninth overall—there were only 22 finishers out of 98 starters in an exceptionally rough and tough four-day non-stop event which was routed deep into the uncivilised interior of Jugoslavia (and, in spite of its title, went nowhere near Rome!)— and it proved to be almost completely reliable.

Starting from Competition Number 78, Gott was always faced with the problem of passing slower competitors on the rough and often dusty tracks and, like all good team captains, he also stopped on more than one occasion to offer help to stranded team-mates. At one point, it was thought that the car had dire engine trouble, as it began misfiring, but this problem was traced to a loose distributor, cured by BMC rally mechanics, and resulted in a far more healthy car. Even though 23 cars had started in the Twin-Cam's capacity class, and although Gott had been told to 'finish at all costs', the Twin-Cam was fourth in its class behind three of the rugged and rally-developed rear-engined Porsches. Not only that, but Gott beat two of the team's four Austin-Healey 100-Six cars which formed BMC's main assault on the Liège that year!

It was a promising start, but from this point luck began to turn against the 'works' Twin-Cams in rallying. The next outing was on the Monte Carlo Rally, in January 1959, by which time the red Coupe had been registered RMO 101, was driven by Gott and Brookes, and started the traditionally snowy event from Glasgow. Compared with the 1958 rally, one so badly affected by snow that it had been something of an achievement even to struggle through to the finish, the 1959 event was much easier, and nearly 70 per cent of the huge (321 car) entry arrived in Monte Carlo on sched-ule. Everything, it seemed, would be settled around the 270-mile mountain circuit, by precise time-keeping. It was a real shock, therefore, for those of us following the fortunes of the event, to hear that Gott had crashed the Twin-Cam on the descent of the Col de Braus, less than an hour after the start of the test. Although the car was not badly bent (it was driven all the way back to Abingdon afterwards), it had slid down a bank after Gott had swerved to avoid a boulder, and was only stopped by a stout sapling. Two trucks were needed to haul it out.

Both cars were re-prepared for the Tulip rally of 1959, with John Gott and Chris Tooley driving PRX 707, the roadster, and John Sprinzel and Stuart Turner driving the repaired Coupe. Neither figured in the awards, and in neither case was it the fault of a Twin-Cam. Both Tooley and Stuart Turner (Turner, of all people, probably the most professional navigator of them all at the time!) made navigational errors, both cars lost a great deal of time, and neither could make up for it.

The following month, BMC tried again, when the Coupe, RMO 101, was entered in the fast and demanding Greek Acropolis Rally, for John Sprinzel to drive. On this occasion his co-driver was Richard Bensted-Smith of *The Motor*, a writer noted for his dry sense of humour, and his calm acceptance of unexpected events. On this occasion he needed it. Not long after the start, and when the oversteering Twin-Cam had been improved by the simple expedient of discarding the second spare wheel carried on the boot lid, Bensted-Smith commented (in a reminiscent feature article) that: 'Somewhere on the way to Kelli there is a place at the bottom of a downhill which looks like a wet right-hand corner until you get closer to it, when it looks like a *sharp* wet right-hand corner with *loose gravel* on the outside....' As wet Greek roads are

For 1960 Ted Lund's Twin-Cam (which was effectively a clandestine 'works' car) was converted to this hardtop specification—screen, doors, and wind-up windows were all normal Twin-Cam Coupe items, but the fast-back style was specially developed for this race (*Autocar*)

incredibly slippery, the result was inevitable. The Twin-Cam flew off into thin air, crashed in a meadow alongside a Porsche which had just completed the same trick, and was joined by two other cars in the next few minutes. There was no escape, and yet another Twin-Cam outing ended in retirement, with the car completely blameless.

After such a disappointing start to the Twin-Cam's rallying career, the Competitions Department discarded it altogether, and disposed of the cars. It was just about the time that the Austin-Healey 100-Six was giving way to the Austin-Healey 3000, and that the development of this fine and rugged machine was coming to fruition. Marcus Chambers could see no further use for the Twin-Cam in rallying, and never used one again.

There was, however, one rather belated postscript to the story. For 1962, having homologated the car on rather flimsy production evidence, Chambers's successor, Stuart Turner, had a 1600 Mk II De Luxe Coupe prepared for rallying. This, of course, was effectively a Twin-Cam Coupe fitted with the 1,622cc pushrod ohv engine, and in this case the engine was fitted with all possible competition equipment including a twin-choke Weber carburettor.

It was used just three times. In the 1962 Monte Carlo Rally, an event where the flat-out stages were mainly dry and little affected by snow, and in which a handicapping system which considered engine capacity was in use, it was driven by the Morley twins, won its (2-litre) capacity class, and finished second overall in the Grand Touring category behind David Seigle-Morris's Abingdon-built Austin-Healey 3000.

In the Tulip Rally, held in May, it was driven by Rauno Aaltonen and Gunnar Palm, and once again won its 2-litre class against a team of three 'works' Triumph TR4s, which had full 2-litre engines. The fact that Aaltonen's test times made him the sixth fastest car in the event did not help, for there was a particularly involved 'class-improvement' handicap in use. The

The rear end of SRX 210, the 'not-quite-works' Twin-Cam which raced at Le Mans between 1959 and 1961. In 1960 and 1961 it had this fastback coupe style, with a central fuel-filler location (*Graham Norman*)

stupidity of it all is illustrated by the fact that Aaltonen finished ahead of the Morley Twins' Big Healey, in spite of the fact that their 3-litre car was the fastest car in the event!

The third and last outing for this Coupe, registered 151 ABL, was the Liège–Sofia–Liège, where John Gott and Bill Shepherd pitted it against the dust, rocks, and impossible time schedules of the world's most difficult rally. Like most of the cars in the event, the MGA was forced to retire, having banged a hole into its fuel tank on two separate occasions. MG lovers (and rally historians) may take heart from the fact that the same fate befell 'works' MGBs in the later events.

As far as the racing of Twin-Cams was concerned, the Competitions Department were somewhat hampered by BMC corporate policy, which stated that there should be no factory involvement in European racing. This did not, however, preclude them from building cars for use by Hambro Automotive in North America. It was something of a tradition, too, that BMC Cars—MGs or Austin-Healeys—should be entered for the most prestigious of North American events, which was the 12-hour Sports Car race at the Sebring airfield circuit.

For 1959, no fewer than four Twin-Cam Coupes were prepared at Abingdon, and sent out to compete in the Sebring race. These were Chassis Numbers 935, 936, 937, and 938, originally built in December 1958. Three cars started, and pictures of the cars in the pits before the start of the race show two to have been 'registered' as PRX 707 and MJB 167. Both were legitimate Abingdon numbers, but if you'll believe the registrations you'll believe anything, for PRX 707 was still a rally car, and was about to do the Tulip Rally, while MJB 167 had originally been registered as an MGA 1500, with pushrod engine, in 1956!

Let's not go into the doubtful legality of using false, or misleading, registration plates on racing cars, but merely record that two cars took second and third places in the 1,600cc Grand Touring class, driven by Gus Ehrman–Ray Saidel–Sherman Decker, and by Jim Parkinson–John Dalton respectively. They should surely be excused for not winning their class, for this was dominated by the very special twin-cam Porsche Carrera of Huschke von Hanstein and Count Carol de Beaufort, which also took second overall in the entire GT category.

A year later, just before the Twin-Cam dropped out of produc-

tion altogether, Sebring was graced with the entry of several Tourers (fitted with aluminium detachable hardtops). No fewer than
five cars were race-prepared at Abingdon (Chassis Numbers 2571
to 2575 inclusive, *very* near the end of the run), three of which
were semi-official entries, registered UMO 94, UMO 95, and
UMO 96 respectively. Messrs Hayes and Leavens were third in
their class, while Parkinson and Flaherty took fourth place.

However, as with rallying, so with racing; the pushrod-engined
1600 De Luxe concept proved to be very useful at Sebring in the
next two years. In March 1961 two Coupes were sent over to the
United States, where they battled throughout the 12-hour event
with the works-prepared Sunbeam Alpines for the 1,600cc class.
Persistence, in the end, was rewarded, for Jim Parkinson and Jack
Flaherty won the class, with Peter Riley, Sir John Whitmore and
Bob Olthoff behind them, in second place. These cars were beauti-
fully prepared, if not outstandingly fast, and featured radiator
grilles reduced in size by a blanking plate, twin air intakes—one
on each side of the grille, like those used as long ago as 1955 on the
TT cars—and the removal of the bumpers.

For 1962, with the 1,622cc MGA 1600 Mk II in production, it
might have been necessary for the cars to be entered in an unsuit-
able class, but Stuart Turner was far too experienced to fall into
that trap. Three new De Luxe Coupes—Chassis Numbers 106073,
106074 and 106075—were built up, from scratch, in the department, but were given modified Mk I style radiator grilles and
special tail lamps, old-type 1,588cc pushrod engines, and called
Mk I De Luxe models! Thus it was that Jack Sears, Andrew
Hedges, Jim Parkinson, Jack Flaherty, Sir John Whitmore and
Bob Olthoff all managed to finish the event running strongly, but
the might of Porsche, and on this occasion the Harper–Procter
Sunbeam Alpine, were too fast for them.

Though the factory was not supposed to be involved in European racing, they wriggled out of this ban. In 1959 a rather special
Twin-Cam was prepared for the Le Mans 24-hour sports car race,
even though it was entered by the North-West Centre of the MG
Car Club. The story behind this car stems from 1956, when Ted
Lund was supposed to be driving a tubular-framed prototype,
having a Twin-Cam engine and a standard-looking light-alloy
body shell. BMC's racing ban put a stop to that, but it was Lund
who eventually persuaded John Thornley to back him in 1959. A

new car, registered SRX 210 (a real giveaway, this, for the 'RX' series of letters were often seen on Abingdon-owned cars) was built up on the basis of a standard Twin-Cam chassis, but with a light-alloy body shell which was part of the 'left over' material from the earlier MGA racing programme. This was of the open variety, and was given the reduced height, full-width, competition windscreen, and an extra carburettor intake on the right.

In 1959 the drivers, Ted Lund and Colin Escott, were out of luck. After completing 185 laps—well over half the distance they could have been expected to notch up during the 24-hour race— they were unfortunate enough to strike a large dog at high speed, which killed the poor animal at once and inflicted great damage to the Twin-Cam's nose and cooling system. Since the car was running with a full-length undertray, and very little hot air could escape from the engine bay or transmission tunnel, it was something of a toss-up as to which failed first. In the end, the gearbox oil boiled, the seals blew, most of the oil was deposited on the undertray, and the transmission seized; the engine was about to boil, and failure could not have been far behind. While running, the Twin-Cam set a fastest lap at 99.47mph, which was little slower than the 160bhp prototype 2-litre twin-cam Triumph TR3Ss, and it had looked to be very reliable.

For the 1960 race, the regulations had been changed, and demanded a much deeper windscreen. Accordingly, it was decided to convert the car into a Coupe, still with all-alloy panels, but with a special fastback body style in which the usual 'bubble-top' roof was swept smoothly down to the tail, to incorporate a large rear window, extra rear quarter windows, and to have a recessed housing for the fuel filler cap. Don Hayter, later to become MG's chief engineer in the late 1970s, was responsible for this.

Ted Lund had now bought the car from the factory, with an engine bored out to 79.4mm (1,762cc) and fitted with two dual-choke Weber carburettors, and running a 4.1:1 axle ratio instead of the original 3.9:1 (the standard car, incidentally, had a 4.3:1 ratio). In the race itself Lund and Escott kept going throughout the 24 hours, finished twelfth out of twenty surviving cars, and averaged 91.12mph. Their fastest lap was at 99.12mph, very slightly slower than in 1959, which tends to support the view that the revised body shell exerted more drag than the original Tourer, although it was still capable of at least 130mph in a straight line.

It is not generally realised, incidentally, that in 1960 the Twin-Cam not only won its class (1,601 to 2,000cc) at Le Mans, but that it also defeated the entire Triumph TRS team of cars—cars which not only had all-aluminium prototype 160bhp engines but glass-fibre body shells not even based on that of a production Triumph. All in all, Ted Lund and Colin Escott put up a remarkable performance.

The fastback Coupe started one more Le Mans race, in 1961, this time with a modified nose style, having headlamps pushed a few inches back into the front wings, and with a much smaller, almost unrecognisable, radiator air intake. The engine power had been boosted to 128bhp, which made the car capable of 140mph. On this occasion, however, the 24-hour race proved too much for the unit. After the car had lapped at 101.66mph, but had completed only 14 laps, the engine threw a connecting rod, and destroyed itself. Ted Lund and his new co-driver, Bob Olthoff, had the doubtful distinction of being the first crew to retire.

Mention of Bob Olthoff, incidentally, brings to the surface his own Twin-Cam Tourer, imported back to Britain in 1960. This had already achieved great success in South Africa (as the very first CKD Twin-Cam to be assembled there) and was used by Olthoff in Europe until the end of 1961. However, even though the young South African took a job at Abingdon for a time, and even though his car was registered as YRX 310 (a local Abingdon number, of course), this was never a 'works' racing car, and should not be considered as such.

However, there is no doubt that Olthoff, once his driving talents became clear, received quite a lot of clandestine support from the MG factory, as indeed did Dick Jacobs (an MG dealer from Woodford, East London) with a couple of Twin-Cam Tourers registered 1MTW and 2MTW. These last two cars won their class in the *Autosport* championships of 1959 and 1960 and won no less than 30 places in 32 events. In view of this, it comes as no surprise to know that Dick Jacobs, who had so nearly lost his life in a Le Mans crash in one of the 1955 prototype MGAs, was one of Abingdon's favourite sons.

The real 'works' competition life of Twin-Cam engined cars was short, however, for once the production car had been discontinued in mid-1960 the factory rather lost interest in it. On the one hand, the Competitions Department had refined the Big Healeys to a high standard of performance and reliability, such that they were potential *and* actual rally winners, and on the other hand the forthcoming unit-construction MGB would not be carrying a Twin-Cam option. And yet, as the record-breaking achievements of EX181 prove, the basic engine had a great deal of potential. It is a great shame that the time never seemed to be ripe for a full-blooded programme of development for the Twin-Cams to take place.

⑤
The Twin-Cam Today

Even though the last MGA Twin-Cam was built at Abingdon in 1960, and even though BMC turned their backs on it almost immediately, MG enthusiasts all over the world never allowed it to become a forgotten car. The Twin-Cam's reputation may have been somewhat shaky while the car was still actually on sale, but it seems to have been improving ever since. More and more Twin-Cams continue to be rebuilt, restored, or even re-constructed, which is a great credit to the specialists who have managed to assemble, or to remanufacture, the parts to make this possible. There is no hope of getting Twin-Cam parts through dealer channels, of course, for BMC stopped supporting its preservation many years ago.

Between 1958 and 1960, a total of 2,111 Twin-Cams were built, but how many of these still survive? It is almost impossible to do more than make an educated guess, but on the evidence available the situation is encouraging. The Twin-Cam Register of the MG Car Club has positively located about 500 genuine Twin-Cams, now known to be on the road (or recently to have been in use) all over the world. It is also known that more are being re-constructed (usually by the reinstatement of a Twin-Cam engine, removed so many years ago), prior to being put back on the road. Since it is now virtually impossible to find new cylinder head or cylinder block castings (at least, not without a long wait, and at great expense), it is something of a miracle that the total stock is slightly increasing, rather than decreasing.

Of those 500 surviving Twin-Cams, perhaps 200 are still in Britain, which is really remarkable, when one considers how few were actually registered here when the model was in current production. Many of the others are in North America (where half the cars were originally delivered), and there is a thin sprinkling in many other countries, notably South Africa, Australia and (of all places) South America.

One or two cars, incidentally, appeared to have been synthesised, and although they have been given Twin-Cam engines and the Twin-Cam wheel and disc brake installations, they are nevertheless not genuine and original Twin-Cams built by MG at Abingdon. Some years ago, the question of originality was not considered important by the buyers of ageing thoroughbred cars, but with the rise of the 'classic car' movement this trend has been sharply reversed. (I mention, merely as an example, a car I inspected not long ago, which its owner said was an MGA 1600 Mk II De Luxe. In fact the car had a Twin-Cam chassis, brakes and wheels, along with a Twin-Cam's removable inner wheel arch panels, but it had an MGA 1600 engine, and a chassis number plate which placed it well before the first of the De Luxes had ever been built, and a number which had nothing whatever to do with the obvious Twin-Cam origins of the chassis!)

Unless a Twin-Cam owner finds a dealer who stocked parts for the MGA Twin-Cam when it was in production, and who has not got rid of the remnants of his old stock, it is highly unlikely that any parts are now available through 'normal channels', either here or in North America. The single significant exception is that certain MGB front suspension parts are the same as those used on the Twin-Cam, and certain others can be modified to do the same job. Even the gearbox internals, which were shared with the earlier MGB models, are now extremely difficult to locate. In every case, incidentally, I would recommend that an owner goes looking for a part *by its part number*, and that he does not mention the Twin-Cam when doing so. The point here is that, invariably, if 'Twin-Cam' is mentioned, then the response from a parts salesman is a blank-faced 'No'. At least if a part number is quoted, he will have to consult his microfilm records to see if any such items still exist.

It would be very easy at this point to start mentioning specialists' names and locations, but as a book like this is likely to stay in print for some time, and as some of these firms may wilt, die away, or close down completely, it would be a counterproductive process. My overall advice, therefore, is that a Twin-Cam owner should try to cultivate the acquaintance of another Twin-Cam owner as soon as possible, so that he can take advice on the suppliers with the most expertise, and the best stocks. He should, in any case, join the major MG owners' club in his particular country. In Britain this is certainly the MG Owners' Club, and in other countries there will usually be a specialist national organisation, either with links to the British MG Car Club Ltd (which is more of a sporting body than one which concerns itself with preservation of olders MGs), or with the MG Owners' Club.

Even though the chassis frames were always extremely sturdy, they can begin to rust away in certain areas, and it is all too easy to distort their alignment when making welding repairs (or after the renovation of a frame following accident damage). It is possible, at great expense, to find new frames in some countries, and it is even possible to modify that of a pushrod-engined MGA to Twin-Cam specification. Incidentally, because the Twin-Cam had a solid separate chassis frame, it almost always provided a feasible base for the 'ground-up' restoration of a badly neglected motor car, whereas the rusty remains of an MGC or an MGB GT V8 monocoque can often be much too far gone to make this possible.

Getting parts for the body shell is feasible, though in many cases patience, shopping around, and a lot of judicious bargaining may be needed. As I have already made clear in an earlier chapter, the panels fitted to a Twin-Cam are sometimes different in subtle ways from those used by pushrod-engined cars, and it is far too easy to be fobbed off with the wrong item by an uncaring or inexpert supplier. Skin panels in general are available, some off new tooling and very accurate, some made by craftsmen's methods. If originality is of no importance to an owner, he can certainly get glass-fibre skin panels, which are a whole lot cheaper than steel panels, but which reduce the eventual re-sale value of the car (and ensure that it can never win prizes in Concours events if the judges are at all alert).

There is really no shortage of decorative items, badges, bright-work and the like, while there is a goodly supply of glass, some new and some secondhand. Even the sharply curved Coupe wind-screen, and the rear windows for the optional 'works' hardtops can be located if you know where to look.

In fact, if the structural basis of the car's body shell is present (preferably in sound condition), a good deal of time, searching around and—inevitably—money will certainly result in the im-maculate restoration of the looks of the machine. There is no problem, incidentally, in obtaining the correct colours, for their formulae are all known, and can be duplicated exactly by the specialists in paint supply.

However, if the body shell and its condition governs the looks of the Twin-Cam, its entire *raison d'être* is bound up in the twin overhead camshaft engine. Although experience tells us that the cylinder block and head of these engines can be surprisingly resistant to frost damage, and to neglect, it is a fact that the light-alloy head might have suffered badly from internal corrosion. Only in one or two places, and then only for a great deal of money, are replacement castings available. All manner of major renovation *can* be carried out on the engine, even including the repair of frost damage to the cylinder head. Most engines have now been converted to the final 8.3 : 1 compression ratio, achieved by the use of lowered-compression pistons. Now that 100-plus octane fuel has virtually disappeared from the world's forecourts, it is recommended that any Twin-Cam rebuild should include this work these days, and that the 9.9 : 1 ratio pistons should be reserved for special fuel blends, and for competitions.

For reliability and durability reasons, it is also recommended that the cylinder head should be converted to the final build specification, which is to say that the long tappets should be fitted, and that the tappet guide sleeves should be inserted into the cylinder head casting itself. All the valve gear items, but not many standard camshafts, are available, and this extends to Renolds drive chains, sprockets, and other related details. Badly worn crankshafts (which are not the same as the pushrod-engined car's crank) can be restored to their former glory, by the redepositing of metal, and by regrinding. Several grades of oversize pistons, incidentally, are available in 8.3 : 1 compression ratio, but it is also quite usual to bore out, then sleeve back, a cylinder block to its original nominal dimension.

The single most difficult area of supply for the engines concerns connecting rods, for which new supplies appear to have dried up. Most surplus stock in the early 1960s, it seems, was used in race-prepared MGA or MGB engines, and no new supplies were manufactured to take their place. The normal MGA 1600 connecting rods are not the same, and are by no means as sturdy for their job.

In general, transmissions can be rebuilt, for the gearboxes had much in common with the pushrod-engined MGAs of the day, and some supplies of new or reconditioned parts can be found both in Britain and in North America. Some cars, incidentally, have been converted from coil spring to diaphragm spring clutches, which is technically advisable, and since the Concours judges cannot see inside the bell housing we see no reason why this should not be done by everyone renovating a Twin-Cam.

The braking system, when in good condition, gives a very good performance, and fortunately it is possible to renovate almost any Twin-Cam's brakes to their rightful state. Supplies of discs are available to replace old ones badly worn or corroded, and Girling (who took over the rights to manufacture Dunlop disc brakes in the mid-1960s) are very helpful indeed in supplying parts for the disc calipers themselves. The calipers are basically the same as those used on several other cars of the 1950s and 1960s (including, for instance, the Jaguar XK150, Mk II saloons and other derivatives, the Jensen 541R and its descendants, and several limited-production European GT cars). A word of warning, however, is that a reconditioned Twin-Cam caliper should be re-assembled *exactly* as it originally was—it might be dangerous, for instance, to use other hydraulic pipe runs which could be vulnerable to flying stone damage; when they arranged the original system, MG engineers knew what they were doing.

The wheels are now extremely difficult to find, although with a great deal of care it is possible to reconstruct Twin-Cam wheels which have been bent by 'kerbing', though this is not recommended in every case. Clearly the rim itself is a standard profile item (and is 4.5 inches wide—*not* the same, incidentally, as that used on the Gordon-Keeble, although that car looks the same), but the centre pressing is very special. Because these wheels feature 'peg drive' they cannot be replaced by normal disc wheels, nor by wire wheels—in any case such a move would destroy the originality of the car being restored or maintained.

Many cars being revived from long neglect and storage need complete electrical renovation, so for Twin-Cam buyers it is good to know that wiring looms, instruments and switchgear are all either available, or can be re-built and repaired. The rev counters, however, had unique markings, and new spares are no longer available, though such instruments (which were mechanically driven from the half-speed shaft on the engine) can be re-built by the instrument specialists in Britain or North America.

In summary, a Twin-Cam is always worth rebuilding if it is mechanically complete, in whatever condition, with the proviso that the engine must be structurally sound. The key to the rejuvenation of Twin-Cams is the engine itself, for as I have made clear there are virtually no supplies of spare castings, and it is highly unlikely that anyone else is going to break a Twin-Cam for spares these days and make another engine available.

The question we have never posed, so far, in this chapter is — is it worth doing at all? And what sort of car do you get when all the work is done? There is a short and very sweet answer to all this — that a properly built, and carefully maintained MGA Twin-Cam is a real joy to own, a thoroughbred by almost any standards. Even with the lower-compression engine, it will be much quicker than any pushrod-engined MGA, quicker than any MGB, quicker *and* better handling than any four-cylinder engined Triumph TR, and a much more desirable car, in almost every way, than the average run-of-the-mill Alfa Giulietta, which was both more common and much more difficult to make structurally sound. It was the only MG ever to be put on sale with a twin overhead camshaft engine, and the only MG ever to have four-wheel disc brakes. It was different, and it was distinctive. The pity of it all was that, at the time it was actually on sale, its reputation was not sufficiently high. Nowadays there are hundreds, if not thousands, of previous Twin-Cam owners who wish they had held on to these interesting cars.

⑥

MGB and MGC
– Six into Four will Go!

Most motoring enthusiasts would agree, I am sure, that the six-cylinder engined MGC was one of the most controversial sports cars ever produced at Abingdon. It was a car which got a mixed reception from the press when it was launched, and it was never short of attention during its short and rather turbulent life. There are grounds, however, for thinking that the MGC was always a much misunderstood car, so a detailed look at its origins are necessary to get the story straight.

First, it must be made absolutely clear that the MGC was not the precise type of new model which MG would have liked to build at the time, but they had little choice. Throughout the 1950s and 1960s, John Thornley and Syd Enever never had a free hand in planning for MG's future. Whether they liked it or not (and, to be fair, they always did their best to put a brave face on it), their policies were always dictated from the BMC headquarters at Longbridge.

The period in which the car which became known as the MGC was conceived was one of the most eventful in BMC's history. At the time, what was happening looked confusing, but a sober backward glance (with the benefit of hindsight) shows that three definite influences were at work. Half-hearted attempts at inter-marque rationalisation were still being made (though the great strides in this policy had all been completed in the 1950s); second, a sales-orientated strategy of wholesale 'badge-engineering' was being pursued with a dedication unmatched by any other British combine; finally, there was the Issigonis-inspired philosophy of producing 'Advanced-Engineering' cars, which was going ahead full-blast.

Work had begun on the definitive successor to the MGA—a car

BMC tried to persuade Donald Healey to lend his name to an Austin-Healey derivative of the new MGC, though he declined to be involved. This is what the 'Austin-Healey 3000 Mk IV' might have looked like (*BL*)

which carried the Abingdon project code of EX205, and a BMC code of ADO23—in 1959, and after a period of uncertainty brought about by the vacillation of engine design policy at Longbridge, and a dispute between MG and Pressed Steel (who were still independent at that stage) over tooling costs, the new car, the MGB, went into production in July 1962. It was the second pressed-steel unit-construction sports car body shell to be put into production by BMC (the little Austin-Healey Sprite of 1958 had been the first), and in packaging terms it was a significant advance over the MGA. Not only did the MGB have a shorter wheelbase (7ft 7in instead of 7ft 10in), but it had considerably more space for the passengers, a lowered floor, a larger boot, and such advanced features as wind-up glass windows in the doors, and the space for two very occasional '+2' seats to be squeezed in behind the front seats for the fastback Coupe version which followed in 1965. Much of the MGB's power train and suspension was developed from that of the MGA. The engine, at 1,798cc, was an enlarged version of the final MGA's 1,622cc, the gearbox, back axle and front suspension were the same as before, and that indefinable quality, 'The Abingdon touch', was present in great quantities. The styling, it was said, had been inspired by that of the mid-engined EX181 record car of 1957, though the two cars were really so different that it could have been no more than a philosophical similarity. The open car, incidentally, was shaped entirely by Abingdon staff (of whom Don Hayter takes much of the credit), while the MGB GT which followed owed much to the ministrations of Pininfarina, who got *their* inspiration from a special-bodied car designed by three Swiss enthusiasts in 1962 on the basis of an Austin-Healey 3000 rolling chassis.

Which brings me neatly to the question of the Austin-Healey 3000—the 'Big Healey' as it was universally known by all its admirers—a very successful car still in full-scale production at Abingdon. It was the *original* Big Healey of 1952 which had so attracted Leonard Lord's attention that he had adopted it for BMC's use, renamed it an Austin-Healey, and frozen out the prototype MGA for a couple of years because he did not want to authorise two new BMC sports cars at the same time. The Big Healeys had been designed and developed by Donald and Geoffrey Healey in Warwick, and had originally been assembled at Longbridge. However, following the centralisation of all BMC sports car assembly, the Big Healey assembly lines were moved to Abingdon in the autumn of 1957.

Soon after the MGB was launched, therefore, Abingdon was bursting at the seams with the production of four distinctly different ranges of cars—the MGBs, the Big Healeys, the Sprite/Midget models, and, would you believe, Morris Minor Travellers (estate cars) and Vans! It was a situation not merely confined to Abingdon, but also to be found at Longbridge, and at Cowley as well. Even at this stage, in 1963 or 1964, BMC's finances were not at all securely underpinned, and further rationalisation was needed in many areas to streamline the production process.

It was in this sort of situation, therefore, that BMC's bosses began to consider the building of a new sports car at Abingdon. They were quite happy with their 'badge-engineered' Austin-Healey Sprites and MG Midgets (and in spite of the fact that no effort was ever made to hide the fact that mechanically these cars were *exactly* the same, both sold very well, and both attracted their own following), but they were becoming rather irritated by the need to build the Big Healey, whose popularity had already passed its peak, and whose structure had absolutely nothing in common with any other BMC model. Nor were they happy in their business relationship with Jensen, who built the body/chassis units for the Big Healeys at their West Bromwich factory before transporting them south to Abingdon for final assembly.

BMC's planners, at this point in history, were not noted for sensitivity, nor for their attachment to the traditions of any BMC marque. Against the better judgement of John Thornley *and* Donald Healey, therefore, they proposed that, when the time came to replace the Big Healey, a new larger-engined car should be developed from the original basis of the four-cylinder MGB model. In this way, it was suggested, Abingdon could get back to assembling just two different sports cars, a new Austin-Healey could be introduced, *and* a larger-engined MG could be announced for the first time since the 1930s. Since the assembly of Morris Minor derivatives was also expected to end in 1964, it all looked logical.

In industrial terms, perhaps, it was logical, but as far as the true enthusiasts at MG and Austin-Healey were concerned, it was nothing to be enraptured about. For a time, however, there was no actual dissent, for the same thing had been done with the Austin-Healey Sprite of 1958 (which became the Mk 2 Sprite and the Mk I MG Midget in 1961), without any lasting harm to reputations, or without too many feathers being ruffled.

The principal problem—engineering, rather than marketing—related to the mechanical transplants which had to take place. It was generally agreed, even by Syd Enever, who would have to oversee the detailed engineering work, that there was a great deal of space under the bonnet of the MGB for a larger engine to be squeezed into place. Even though he had never planned it that way, the 1,798cc four-cylinder engine of the MGB fitted so compactly into place, with the water radiator close up in front of it, that there were several inches of fresh air ahead of the radiator, and immediately behind the grille. On the basis that any re-engining would have to be done without destroying the weight distribution or handling balance of the basic MGB, an 'engine transplant' looked to be a practical proposition.

86

The question was—what engine? It was not as simple as it sounded. The first point was that the big six-cylinder engine currently fitted to Big Healeys was not considered ideal, while the available alternatives were conspicuous by their absence. In his own books, Geoffrey Healey has confirmed that a return to a refined version of the *four*-cylinder 2.6-litre Austin-Healey engine (using the 100S type of cylinder head) was suggested and rejected, and that a plan to use BMC-Australia's six-cylinder engine (a development of the four-cylinder B-Series engine, and built only in Australia) was also abandoned in the face of too many practical and economic difficulties. No other engines were available; the 4-litre Austin Princess unit was far too bulky, and ancient in design, while the 4-litre Rolls-Royce Princess R was not yet thought suitable for sports car use. The new project—coded ADO51 for the 'Austin-Healey' version, and ADO52 for the 'MG'—therefore came into existence without a definitely available engine.

Two factors then conspired to make another engine available. MG engineers tried—and failed—to persuade the existing 3-litre Big Healey engine to fit under the sleek bonnet of the MGB, while at the same time the Austin designers at Longbridge started to look seriously at the idea of a new big saloon car to replace the Austin A110/Wolseley 6/110 models. It soon became clear that a much revised six-cylinder 3-litre engine was needed, and BMC approval was gained for this.

At this point, another delve back into BMC history is needed. BMC's supremo, Leonard Lord, had instituted a radical engine policy as early as 1952. Of the three BMC engines chosen to be fitted to all quantity-production cars later in the 1950s, the largest was the new in-line six-cylinder unit, the C-Series, which was designed at the Morris Engines Branch in Coventry. Introduced in 1954 as a 2,639cc unit, and with four main crankshaft bearings, it was enlarged to 2,912cc in 1959, and was fitted to several BMC models in one form or another, including (from the autumn of 1956) the Big Healey. To go with it, a new gearbox, and a new hypoid bevel back axle, were also designed and these, too, found a home in the Big Healey. (In the same way, therefore, as the MGB was obliged to use the 'corporate' B-Series power-train, the Big Healey used C-Series units.)

The large quantity-production BMC saloons current when the ADO51/ADO52 project got under way were the Austin West-

(*Above*) The engine fitted to the MGC (and, in all major respects, to the Austin 3-litre of 1968-71) was still of 2,912cc, but different in every way from the older 2,912cc engine used in the Big Healey (*BL*)

(*Below*) The new MGC engine, complete with its gearbox in non-overdrive form. In traditional BMC fashion, all the important electrical components are grouped at the same side of the unit (*BL*)

For comparison purposes only, this is the engine/gearbox assembly of the last of the Big Healeys, the BJ8 model of 1964-8. A look at the MGC's engine (*opposite*), then a check back with this design, shows that almost every detail of the MGC engine was different (*BL*)

minster A110 and the Wolseley 6/110 models, both being 'badge-engineered' derivatives of the same basic design. Styled by Pininfarina in 1957, they had been introduced in 1959, and were due for replacement later in the 1960s.

So far, so good, and this is where the MGC story really starts. Work started on a 'new' Austin 3-litre design as early as 1963, when it was decided to engineer a front-engine/rear-drive large car on the basis of the still-to-be-announced BMC 1800's *front*-wheel-drive body shell. However, as this car was to be the latest of the BMC 'Advanced Engineering' models, it was decided to give it all-independent hydrolastic suspension, self-levelling at the rear—and that a new six-cylinder engine should be developed. The existing C-Series unit was, by then, considered to be too agricultural, and not nearly refined enough.

The 'new' unit—I use the word in inverted commas because it was more truly an extensive re-design of the C-Series engine, by the same designers at Morris Engines, rather than a brand new unit—evolved around two principal requirements, and with several other major considerations to be satisfied. It had to be

89

physically smaller and considerably lighter than the C-Series, and it had to take account of the various exhaust pollution limitations being proposed around the world, and particularly in North America. It also had to be more refined than the C-Series, which almost automatically meant that it would have to be equipped with a seven-bearing crankshaft.

John Thornley and Syd Enever, as I have already made clear, had to accept this 'new' engine with good grace, or as much grace as they could muster. They were happy to try for such a demanding 'shoe-horn' job, on the understanding that the engine was going to be considerably shorter and (preferably) more squat than before, and that it was going to be considerably lighter than the old C-Series. Both considerations were bound up in the advance of casting technology since the C-Series had been designed in 1952/ 1953; cylinder walls could be thinner, as could main engine casting areas, and everything could be shuffled up that important bit closer than before.

Inescapably, however, the engine, which was slated to have a cast-iron cylinder block and head to keep material costs to an absolute minimum, *was* going to be a lot heavier than the B-Series engine, and a lot of development work would still be needed at Abingdon to get back to appropriate MG standards of handling. The tragedy, as far as MG enthusiasts were concerned, was that Morris Engines Branch never managed to get the weight down to the levels they had promised in the first place. At no less than 567 lb the new 3-litre engine, which retained the same bore, stroke, and 2,912cc capacity of the obsolete C-Series, was 209lb heavier than the four-cylinder B-Series engine. The actual weight saving was a mere 20lb, and John Thornley has often said that an extra 50lb saving would have made a marvellous difference to the entire concept.

Like the C-Series engine which it displaced (but unlike the B-Series, of course), the new 3-litre engine had its carburettors and manifolding on the near side of the car, with its camshaft, pushrod valve gear, distributor and all other electrical ancillaries on the right. The overall saving in length, incidentally, was about $1\frac{3}{4}$in— enough, but not comfortably enough, to allow it to be squeezed into place under the MGB's bonnet, but only after a large bulge in the bonnet to fair over the radiator, and an extra small bulge to provide clearance over the forward of the two SU carburettors, had also been provided.

Although all the accumulated development experience of the C-Series engine was available to them, and although the same basic cam profile and valve gear were used again, the Morris Engines designers had not been able to make the new engine as powerful as the Austin-Healey 3000 Mk III unit which it effectively replaced. The comparative figures were as follows:

Engine	Maximum Power	Maximum Torque
Austin-Healey 3000	150bhp (nett) at 5,250rpm	173lb ft at 3,000rpm
New 'MGC' 3-litre	145bhp (nett) at 5,250rpm	170lb ft at 3,400rpm

There were two reasons for the reduction in outputs. One was that the seven-bearing crankshaft gave a minor, but significant, increase in rotating friction and windage, and the other was that certain minor changes made to the cylinder head and combustion chamber, due to impending exhaust emission legislation, had certainly helped to 'clean up' the exhaust gases, but done nothing for the engine's overall efficiency. This, incidentally, was a phenomenon to which the whole world's motor manufacturers were to become accustomed in future years.

Compared with the original MGB, the new car also had entirely different gearbox and back axle installations, but compared with the latest MGB, which was due to be launched at the same time as the new six-cylinder MG, there was a great deal more commonality. The original MGB had used the four-speed gearbox from the MGA, which had a non-synchronised bottom gear, and which was basically the same box as used behind every other B-Series engine in every B-Series BMC motor car.

For the new large Austin ADO61 saloon, and for the six-cylinder engined MG, an entirely new gearbox was designed, with synchromesh for all forward gears. Like the original type of C-Series boxes (but not like the gearbox used on Big Healeys since the end of 1961), the new design had its gear selectors at the side of the casing, with an access panel in that near side, and there were two different sets of internal ratios. Because they had to mate with different clutches, and different cylinder blocks, the gearbox casings of the MGB Mk II (as the 1968-model car was to be known) and the six-cylinder MG were very different in detail, but in all other basic features they were the same. As with the original MGB a Laycock overdrive was optional equipment.

Since the old C-Series axle was due to go out of production when the Big Healey, the Austin A110 and the Wolseley 6/110 were dropped, and since a robust Salisbury type of axle had already been specified for the MGB GT (and, from mid-1967, for the MGB Tourer as well) it was decided to use this for the six-cylinder car.

All this, of course, is to skim over the personal and political ferment caused by the decision to go ahead with a new model having the Austin-Healey and MG badges. For a long time while the car was being developed, it was agreed that the MG should be called MGC (which was entirely logical, for it was a development of the MGB), and that the Austin-Healey version should be the 3000 Mk IV. This, by the way, is not merely wishful thinking and rumour on my part. There is concrete evidence in the design office records (in regard to modifications, and additions to the specification in the years before production began) that this was so. The Healey family—Donald and his son Geoffrey, who actually did most of the detail design of the famous Big Healey—were never happy about this. They had always wanted to go their own way with a Big Healey replacement (a widened version with the 3,909cc Rolls-Royce Princess R FB60 engine was one very strong contender) but had been overruled by BMC. In his splendid book, *Austin-Healey* (published by Gentry Books), Geoffrey Healey has this to say:

> BMC tried very hard to persuade DMH to agree to his name being used on ADO51. A number of attempts were made to upgrade the car to a form that was acceptable, but all left one with the feeling that the one-piece classic design of the MGB had been butchered to produce a mediocre sports car. . . . I spent a lot of time with Syd Enever on the project, and though he did everything possible to make a success out of it, I felt that he realised that it was not the way to go. Perhaps if DMH had agreed to his name going on the car, extra development funds might have been made available. . . . As things turned out, however, DMH was undoubtedly right to refuse to have his name connected. . . .

Whether or not Donald Healey was right to turn down this extension of his links with BMC is not for me to say. What seems to be certain, however, is that it caused some delay to the project. Not, that is, that the MGC could have been put on sale any earlier than it was, for the simple reason that engine supplies could not have been available before the autumn of 1967.

The time-table concerning the concept, development, and eventual production of the six-cylinder MGC confirms that ADO51/ADO52 was not a project which had an easy and untroubled passage through the various processes which have to be surmounted in the volume-production manufacture of cars:

1960: First thoughts on large-engined BMC successor to Austin-Healey 3000

1963: Decision to build 'new' straight-six-cylinder engine for BMC passenger cars

1964: Design work began on MGC, as conversion/update of MGB

1965: First prototype of MGC built

1966: (Autumn) Austin-Healey version finally abandoned
(November) First track-built pre-production MGCs built at Abingdon

1967: (July) Quantity-build of MGCs began
(October) MGC revealed to the public
(December) End of quantity-production of the Big Healey

Getting the MGC into production, however, was by no means as straightforward a process as usual, for building the car was not merely a case of shoe-horning a six-cylinder engine into the body-shell of a four-cylinder car. Much more than this was involved; in the end, the MGC turned out to be something of a complete re-design of the front half of the MGB, and the changes affected the four-cylinder MGB as well. This technical analysis of what was a fascinating 'conversion job', however, belongs to the next chapter.

⑦
MGC – The Technical Analysis

At the same time as the six-cylinder MGC was launched, in October 1967, a revised version of the four-cylinder MGB was also put into production. Since the changes made to the MGB were being carried out so that it could be rationalised with the MGC as far as possible, and since certain MGB changes with that in mind had already taken place, I ought to start by reviewing the way in which the MGB's career had progressed from 1962 to 1967.

The original MGB had entered production in the summer of 1962, when it took over from the long-running and very popular MGA. The MGA had used a massively strong separate chassis frame, and a separate steel body, whereas the MGB's structure was a unit construction, pressed-steel, body chassis unit, and at first it was built at the Morris Bodies Branch in Coventry, from pressings and sub-assemblies supplied from the Pressed Steel Company Ltd's factory at Swindon, in Wiltshire. (The roads in the Cotswolds, therefore, were treated to the sight of fleets of lorries driving north from Swindon to Coventry with pressings, sub-assemblies and complete floor pans for the MGB, and to the sight of other lorries then transporting complete painted and trimmed shells back down the same roads to Abingdon, which was a mere 26 miles from Swindon!)

Almost all the power train, transmission and suspension systems were taken from the MGA. The engine itself was a 1,798cc version of the famous BMC B-Series design, and at this stage the capacity was not shared with any other BMC car or light van. The gearbox was essentially that of the MGA, which is to say that it had an unsynchronised first gear, and in most respects (like the use of common casings, and, as far as possible, gears, bearings, and selector linkages) it was the same as used on several other BMC saloons equipped with B-Series running gear. The major difference, for the MGB, was that a Laycock overdrive was made available as an option, a feature never provided on the MGA. The axle casing itself, the differential gears, and the final drive, were all B-Series items out of the standardised BMC parts bin, and none the worse for that; for the unmodified MGB application they were perfectly adequate. Apart from minor up-dating changes, and a reduction in spring rates, the front suspension, its linkages, damper layout, and even the pressed steel cross-member (which bolted up to the main body shell) were virtually the same as those of the MGA.

The MGB went into production in this form during 1962, but by 1963 certain major developments were under way, not the least of which was that a fastback GT body derivative was being developed, and that BMC had decided to adopt the 1,798cc B-Series engine for the front-wheel-drive 1800 saloon, and at the same time to modify it to include a five-bearing, rather than a three-bearing, crankshaft. The five-bearing MGB engine, which was slightly less powerful than the original three-bearing engine, but never by enough to induce BMC to quote revised power and torque figures, went into production in the autumn of 1964.

By the time the MGB GT, a sleek and extremely civilised 2+2 seater (or that is what the advertising claimed, anyway) Coupe, complete with a glass hatchback, came on to the scene at Abingdon in the autumn of 1965, MG management and designers already knew that a six-cylinder derivative of the basic design would eventually be produced. This explains why the Salisbury type of rear axle was used under the structure of the MGB GT right from the start; the existing B-Series back axle, if suitably prepared and, if necessary, modified, could have dealt with the unchanged power output of the MGB GT, and with the extra 160lb dead weight of the structure. Specifying the Salisbury type of axle, which had a sturdy centre casting and outer steel tubes, rather than the transverse pressed 'banjo' construction of the B-Series axle, therefore not only gave MG experience of the more robust unit, but it also allowed them to balance any supply difficulties caused by the still burgeoning demand for the elegant and versatile MGB.

Indeed, even before series production of MGCs began, the Salisbury axle was also standardised under the structure of the MGB open Tourer, this change taking place in the early summer of 1967. By the autumn of 1967, therefore, the old B-Series 'banjo' axle casing had disappeared from the scene at Abingdon, even though it remained in use on other BMC cars for some time. All MGCs, and MGBs built alongside them, used the same Salisbury-style hypoid axle, its differential, casing, and its high tensile side tubes. Only the variety of final drive ratios were different.

As already explained in the previous chapter, the 2,912cc C-Series engine fitted to Austin-Healey 3000s could not be fitted to the car which was to become the MGC. The 'new' 2,912cc six-cylinder engine developed specifically for the MGC, and for the ADO61 Austin 3-litre, was shorter, a little lighter, and somewhat more compact than before—but it was still a bulky unit. The bulk, and the weight, of the new engine had far-reaching effects on the structure of the car; by the time the MGC had to be tooled up for quantity production, its body shell was much different from that of the MGB, much more special than its sponsors had originally hoped it would be.

Visually, and externally, the MGC's body shell could only be distinguished by the unique shape of the light-alloy bonnet skin panel. If it had not been for the need to clear the water radiator—which had, perforce, been moved well forward of the original MGB position to allow the long six-cylinder engine to be slotted into place—the broad bulge originating at the back of the bonnet might not have needed to be so prominent, but there would still have been a need for some sort of bulge, as the extra blister over the forward carburettor of the engine itself confirms. Apart from this, there was no badging at the front to identify the car from its four-cylinder relative. At the rear, in fact, the only way in which the two cars could be distinguished (apart, that is, from the higher ride height brought on by the larger wheels, the reason for which is described below) was by the badging on the boot-lid (Tourer) or hatchback (GT) panels, and even this difference was discreetly confined to the use of 'MGC' in the badge in place of 'MGB'— just a single letter to be changed.

Under the skin, the changes were so extensive that they effectively resulted in a new floor pan, and Pressed Steel claimed the credit for assembling the complete shells. There was an MGC open Tourer on the Pressed Steel display at Earls Court in 1967, and an MGC GT in 1968.

Because of the length and bulk of the six-cylinder engine, whose front end was several inches ahead of the line of the front wheels

Front suspension detail of the MGC, with Girling disc calipers, telescopic dampers and different suspension links from the four-cylinder MGB. The bolt-on hubs provided for the mounting of centre-lock wire wheels are obvious (*BL*)

rather than just above it as was the four-cylinder MGB unit, and whose oil sump had to find *somewhere* to live, the MGB's cross-member could not be retained. This, and the fact that the so-called 'light-weight' six-cylinder engine was 209lb heavier than the MGB unit (and most of this extra weight was concentrated over the front wheels), made a wholesale re-design of the front suspension necessary. The result was that entirely new inner wheel arch panels (or engine bay valances, if you will—though MG Parts Books call them wheel arches) were designed, and these were mated to a massive new U-shaped front suspension cross-member, which swooped up on each side of the engine from underneath the sump, and carried mountings for the new front suspension, as well as large pads ready to accept the forward engine mountings fixed to each side of the cylinder block.

An MGC development car on the ramp at Abingdon, showing the obviously different torsion-bar front suspension, sump, and exhaust-system layout of the big six-cylinder-engined car (*BL*)

The front suspension itself was entirely special, not at all related to the MGA of MGB suspension assemblies, and was never used on any subsequent derivative of the MGB. In place of the coil spring, lever-arm damper and wishbone system used in the MGB, the MGC used two-piece upper and lower forged wishbones, longitudinal torsion bars, and telescopic dampers. In a singularly elegant mechanical fashion, upper and lower wishbones and the telescopic dampers all pivoted from the new cross-member. The torsion bar itself was splined at each end. The front end was fitted into the rear pivot of the lower wishbone, while the rear end was anchored at an adjustable pivot at the side of the gearbox/propeller shaft tunnel, under the front of the passenger seats of the car. The adjustment was provided, Jaguar fashion, by bolts which could be locked to the pivots, and which abutted against the chassis/body structure itself.

The new front suspension and cross-member/inner wheel-arch combination had to have new 'chassis' side members, and new forward floor panels (under the occupants' legs) to suit. And this

This overhead shot emphasises why it was necessary to push the radiator of the MGC well forward compared with the MGB position. Cosmetically, this shot is not absolutely correct, for there is no 'MG' badge on the rocker cover (*BL*)

all meant that the entire hidden 'inner front end' of the MGC's body shell was different from that of the four-cylinder MGB, though from a point under the seats to the tail of the car there was no important difference, nor were the doors, the principal scuttle/bulkhead panels, or the instrument layout affected.

In many ways, the Type 29G 2,912cc engine was very similar indeed to that of the ADO61 Austin 3-litre (though that car did not enter series production until the late summer of 1968). Indeed, the most knowledgeable MGC enthusiasts often buy the remains of an Austin 3-litre (which most assuredly is *not* worth preserving) so that they can use the engine and gearbox out of that car, when necessary, to provide parts for the rebuilding of an MGC (which is worthwhile). The main features, such as the cast-iron cylinder block and head, the seven-bearing crankshaft, many auxiliaries, and even the inlet manifold are common, as is most of the valve gear. When the Austin 3-litre was announced in 1967 it had 8.2:1 compression ratio pistons, but by the time series production seriously got under way in 1968 the ratio had been raised to 9.0:1 and the pistons were therefore commonised with those of the MGC.

Peak performance ratings, however, were very different, which points to the use of a different camshaft profile, and other details, for the MGC, even though the same $1\frac{3}{4}$in choke SU HS6 carburettors were employed. The MGC's peak figures were 145bhp (nett) at 5,250rpm, and 170lb ft of torque at 3,400rpm; for the Austin 3-litre in production form, the peak power was 124bhp (nett) at 4,500rpm, and 161lb ft of torque at 3,000rpm.

As far as the MGC was concerned, the camshaft used was the same for every market destination, including North America, though there were important differences to the cylinder head, inlet and exhaust manifolds, and carburation. For North America, there was an entirely special inlet manifold, with equal length pipes from the carburettor flanges to cylinder head face, and without any type of gallery; to facilitate this, the spacing of the carburettors was increased by 2.0in. The exhaust manifolds, too, were different, and had complete hot-spotting attachments to the inlet manifolds to assist rapid warm-up from cold, and to minimise exhaust emissions. As far as the carburettors themselves were concerned, for North America all manner of mixture control devices were needed, and there was a belt-driven air pump mounted on the opposite side of the engine from the electrical alternator (and using a separate drive belt) which squirted air into the exhaust ports to encourage complete combustion before the exhaust gases reached the outside world.

Although there were considerable detail differences between the USA-specification engines (which were coded 29GA, where A stood for America in BMC systems language) and those built for delivery to the rest of the world, the USA engine did not seem to have suffered any noticeable diminution in its overall performance abilities. A study of the performance figures published in *Road & Track* for an MGC tested in the United States confirms that this was so.

Now it is time to consider the transmission layout, and first I must draw comparisons with the MGB, and I must also be precise as to my definitions. I will start by making the obvious, and obviously correct, statement that the *original* B-Series MGB gearbox (which had an unsynchronised first gear) was fitted from 1962 to 1967 to four-cylinder MGBs. I will then follow it up with the slightly more contentious remark, that the Mk II MGB, introduced at Chassis No G/HN4-138800 (Tourer) and G/HD4-139284 (GT), had an all-synchromesh gearbox which was basically the same as that specified for the MGC.

It all depends, you see, by what is meant by 'basically the same'. The situation was as follows. For the new ADO61 Austin 3-litre, and for the closely related MGC, BMC decided that a new all-synchromesh gearbox should be developed. This was to have no relation to the existing large-car C-Series box which in the early and mid-1960s was in use on Austin A110s, Wolseley 6/110s and the Austin-Healey 3000, and also had a non-synchronised first gear, which had been re-jigged in autumn 1961 to have its selector mechanism mounted on top of the casing. The new gearbox was to have all-new details, a higher torque capacity, and was to revert to the use of gear selectors on the left side of the main casing. Like the obsolescent B-Series box, too, it was to have a rather long and complex linkage to the remote-mounted gear lever, through the medium of a secondary linkage inside a remote-control housing. There would be one major gearbox casing, integral with the bell housing cover, a casing which would be commonised between Austin 3-litre and MGC applications.

BMC then decided to up-date the MGB, so that from the autumn of 1967 it, too, could have an all-synchromesh gearbox.

Table 7.1 *MGC Gearbox—Internal Ratios*

Model	Internal ratios	Comment
MGC, non-overdrive (1968 model-year)	1.00, 1.382, 2.167, 3.44, reverse 3.095:1	Used on cars up to Chassis No 4235 (Tourer), and 4234 (GT). Also used on all Mk II and subsequent MGBs, with or without overdrive, and on early-model Austin 3-litre saloons built to end 1968
MGC, overdrive (all models, 1967–1969)	(0.82), 1.00, (1.07), 1.307, 2.058, 2.98, reverse 2.679:1	
MGC, non-overdrive (1969 model-year)	1.00, 1.307, 2.058, 2.98, reverse 2.679:1	Used on all MGCs from chassis No 4236 (GT) and 4266 (Tourer). Also commonised, and used on later-model Austin 3-litre saloons.
—also— MGB Mk II, overdrive—all models	(0.82), 1,00, (1.13), 1.382, 2.167, 3.44, reverse 3.095:1	All overdrive MGB Mk IIs to 1980

Because this car was to retain the B-Series engine, which had different flywheel facing machining details, and because the four-cylinder car did not need anything as robust as a 9in diaphragm spring clutch, it would need an entirely different casing/bell housing cover. Thus it is that, although many of the integral details in the MGC and MGB gearboxes are the same, the gear shaft centres are the same, the selector linkages, remote controls, rear extensions and overdrive adaptors are all the same the principal casing is different and—in some cases—the gear ratios themselves are different. Both types of car—MGB Mk II and MGC—could be supplied with Laycock overdrive, which fixed behind the main gearbox, and which operated on top and third gears in each case. An electrical inhibitor switch, operating on the gear selector linkage through the top of the remote control housing, made sure that overdrive was automatically put out of action when other gears were engaged; this was to ensure that excess torque, which could be transmitted by the gearbox in these gears, did not damage the overdrive itself.

The situation regarding gearbox ratios is somewhat complex, not only because there were two different sets for the MGC at first, but also because one of the sets was later discontinued as far as the MGC was concerned, but was continued for the MGB itself! The rationalisation so far as the MGC was concerned took place at the start-up of the substantial changes made for 1969-model-year cars. Table 7.1 shows these changes in tabular form and indicates the other models on which the ratios were used.

There was really no sensible reason why two different sets of internal gearbox ratios should be specified—particularly as the alteration in third gear and second gear figures was only five per cent—and especially as there could have been no practical production reason why BMC's Tractors and Transmissions factory in Birmingham should enjoy having to machine and assemble two different sets.

However, speaking as an engineer who has worked in the design and development side of the motor industry at various times, I see this as betraying the interest which some technician took in the *overall* bottom gear to be found in the MGC. The reasoning goes like this. At first, non-overdrive cars were fitted with axle ratios of 3.07:1, while overdrive cars were fitted with 3.31:1 ratios. This was done to strike a balance between acceleration capabilities, and

'Hello Big Brother', 'Hello Little Brother'. The MGC GT, complete with 15in wire wheels, a bonnet bulge and more ground clearance, is on the left; the four-cylinder MGB GT, with 14in wheels, on the right (*Autocar*)

the rev-limit of the new engine when approaching maximum speed. However, on the assumption that first, or bottom, gear was just about right for overdrive cars, this might have meant that a non-overdrive car *fitted with those ratios* would have had a bottom gear too high to provide satisfactory hill-start or low speed acceleration capabilities. It is in such a way that ideal straight-line performance is compromised by practical considerations.

During the early life of the MGC, MG development engineers completely re-thought the entire philosophy of the drive line and gearing of the car, especially in the face of initial press comment, which suggested that the car did not build up speed as rapidly as hoped. Except for the cars fitted with automatic transmission (and I will be detailing this transmission shortly), it was decided to lower the gearing of all other MGCs, so that a touch more acceleration could be provided at the expense of relaxed high-speed/low engine speed cruising. It was at this juncture that the 'hill-start'

conundrum dissolved, so that it became possible to commonise on the 'closer-ratio' gear set for manual *and* overdrive MGCs. This change took effect with the start-up of 1969-model-year cars which were altogether better, in many details, than the original variety. (It was precisely because no such changes were being made to the four-cylinder MGB, and indeed never were, that the MGB continued to use the wider-ratio gear set until the day it finally died in 1980.) Borg Warner three-speed automatic transmission, complete with torque converter, was always an option on the MGC. Such a transmission had never before been available on any MG, whether sports car or saloon, because MG (and BMC) had always been quite convinced that there was no demand for it. The times, however, were a-changing, and even in Europe there were people prepared to buy a fast and relatively expensive sports car if they could also drive it with the least possible effort; to such people, the pleasures of using a short, precisely-operating, light manual gear-change were not apparent.

MG, and BMC, therefore, took a deep breath and decided to

make a Borg Warner automatic optional, not only on the MGC but on the MGB Mk II which would be phased in alongside it. The automatic box was more bulky than either the old B-Series manual box or the new manual gearbox, and necessitated a bigger and more spacious tunnel than before. The selector lever for the automatic transmission on these cars was placed on top of the transmission tunnel, in place of the conventional gear lever, and had a P-R-N-D-L_2-L_1 quadrant.

Because the automatic transmission provided the bonus of considerable torque multiplication to counteract the fact that it had only three forward gears, MG were happy to provide the automatic MGC with the same final drive ratio as that of the *original* overdrive car, and this was never altered throughout the life of the car. Even so, I ought to summarise the final drive situation as follows:

Final Drive ratio	*Used on:*
3.07:1	Non-overdrive cars *up to* Ch No 4235
3.31:1	Overdrive cars *up to* Ch No 4235.
	Non-overdrive cars *from* Ch No 4236
	All automatic transmission cars
3.7:1	Overdrive cars *from* Ch No 4236

These axle ratios were the same, no matter for which market a car was destined. It is also relevant, but not too appropriate to normal road cars, that there was a whole variety of optional crown-wheel-and-pinion ratio sets available for this Salisbury axle—in the case of MGBs and MGCs, for competition purposes. These included 3.58, 3.91, 4.22, 4.55, and 4.875:1—the last being a real 'stump puller' only suitable for hill-climbing or for really tight racing circuits.

Compared with the four-cylinder MGB, the other main areas of difference were the steering gear, the brakes, and the road wheels. The least controversial of these areas was that of the brakes. Although the conventional (to MG) mixture of front wheel discs and rear drums was retained, the supplier was changed to Girling (Lockheed supplied brakes for the four-cylinder MGB, and there had been four-wheel Dunlop discs on the MGA Twin-Cam). The front discs themselves were slightly larger in diameter—11.06in instead of 10.75in—whereas the rear drums were smaller in diameter but with wider shoes—9 × 2.5in compared with 10×1.75in for the MGB. On British-market cars there was a single hydraulic circuit, with a vacuum servo remotely mounted on the toeboard bulkhead, whereas on North American ('Federal') cars there were dual circuits, and two vacuum servos, one on the bulkhead, and one fixed to the right-side inner wheel arch panel, close to the oil filter on that side of the engine.

Because the MGC, by definition, was much faster than the MGB, but much heavier into the bargain, a change in tyre specification was mandatory. The MGB's maximum speed was just over 100mph, while that of the MGC was around 120mph. This, among other things, meant that the MGB's tyre rating could not be used, as 'HR' tyres are required for a car with a maximum speed above 180kph, or 112mph. At the time, the tyres specified for MGBs were 5.60–14in cross-plys of 'SR' rating.

For the MGC, radial ply tyres of 165in section were clearly desirable, on engineering, marketing and performance grounds. Such tyres, on a 14in diameter rim, like that of the MGB, were already available—the most noteworthy customer being Rover, for the 2000 model. A high-speed (HR) rating tyre was also available, or was about to be so, for Rover would be retaining the same wheels and rim sections for the vee-8-engined car—the 3500 model—due to enter production early in 1968. MG, however, looked at the traditional use of 15in wheels on the Austin-Healey 3000, which the MGC was going to replace, at the revving capability of the new six-cylinder engine, and at the likely maximum speed of the new car, and chose 15in diameter rims, either disc wheels with five-stud fixing, or centre-lock wire-spoke wheels, with 165–15in, HR rating, Dunlop SP41 radial ply tyres.

The MGC's tyre section, therefore, was the same as that optional on MGB GTs (but with 14in rims), which meant that the size of the tyre contact patch was also approximately the same. It was inevitable, therefore, that the heavier front end weight of the MGC on the same area of rubber would result in greater steering efforts being required by the driver, and in greater front tyre slip angles having to be developed to produce a given turning effect on the car itself. No matter what the most avid MGC lovers will protest, this was a built-in guarantee of increased understeer.

No doubt if the MG designers had had their own way, they would have dealt with it by making further revisions to the car, by altering the front suspension geometry, or at least by using wider

(*Above*) The well-used MGC road-test car of 1967, as used by *Autocar* in manual-plus-overdrive form, to be compared with (*below*) the same magazine's automatic-transmission car of 1968. By this time there was a stowage tray by the passenger's legs, and a swivelling map light under the facia in the centre of the car (*both Autocar*)

wheel rims and larger-section tyres. But—as ever—the question of cost-savings were considered more important, and this was never carried out.

At this stage, and since the question of wheel loading is so important to a consideration of the MGC's road behaviour, I ought to make a few comparisons with the four-cylinder MGB, and with the superseded Austin-Healey 3000. Here, taken from *Autocar's* authoritative road tests, are front/rear weight figures for unladden cars:

Car and Model Year	Front End Weight	Rear End Weight
MGC Tourer (1968)	1,380lb	1,097lb
MGB Tourer (1965)	1,120lb	1,008lb
Austin-Healey 3000 Mk III (1964)	1,354lb	1,250lb

The interesting comparison is that the MGC only carried about 25lb more over its front wheels than the last of the Austin-Healey 3000s had done, whereas it was 260lb heavier in that area than the MGB. This reflects not only the increased weight of the MGC's engine compared with the MGB, but the more forward position it occupied in the body shell compared with both the other cars.

To counteract the effect of the increased weight on steering efforts, if not on the balance of the handling, the MGC was not only given lower-geared steering, but there was also a reduction in the castor in the front suspension geometry. Once again, and for two different reasons, this helped to create the impression of understeer—the lower-geared rack because the steering wheel had to be rotated more to get the same movement of the road wheels, and the de-castored front suspension helping to reduce the self-centring action of the steering, and therefore making it feel more dead and unresponsive.

The steering wheel itself, incidentally, was unchanged at 16.5in diameter (but with leather-covered rim), but on the MGC there were 3.5 turns from lock to lock of a 35-foot turning circle, compared with 2.9 turns lock to lock of a 32-foot turning circle with the MGB. (Few observers, incidentally, ever compare these figures with those of the last variety of Austin-Healey 3000, which had 1,354lb over its steered wheels, a huge 17in diameter steering wheel, 3.0 turns lock to lock, cam and peg steering—and a comment from *Autocar* in their road test of June 1964 that it was *heavy at low* speeds. The italics are mine.)

I will not labour the point at this stage, for the question of the MGC's handling, and the reputation it gained with the press and the public, belongs in the next chapter, except to say that I share the same technical opinion as several other engineers, which was that the designers of the MG were well and truly backed into a corner by a combination of excess engine weight, severe cost and development limitations, the need to commonise with the up-rated MGB as far as possible, and by sheer expediency. With hindsight, it is easy to suggest that the problem could have been alleviated with a lighter engine, with more sophisticated suspension geometry, and with power-assisted steering. Power-assisted steering? Why not? It was technically feasible, for the basic MGC engine was also used in the ADO61 Austin 3-litre, which was already fitted with a belt-driven hydraulic pump to supply fluid to the car's Cam Gears power-assisted steering. In those days, however, it was simply 'not done' to have power-assisted steering on a European sports car (even if the Americans were quite happy to accept it on their own Chevrolet Corvettes) and the extra on-cost would probably have ruled it out of court in any case.

So far in this chapter I have made little mention of the trim and furnishing specification of the MGC, not because it was not worthy of attention, but because it was almost exactly the same as that of the uprated MGB Mk II introduced at the same time. The body style options—open Tourer, or fastback hatchback GT— were the same, as were the seating arrangements. The Tourer was a two-seater, with substantial stowage space behind the seats, whereas the GT had the familiar 2 + 2 seating, where the rear seat leg room was virtually nil, and where the rear seat's backrest could be folded down to increase the length (and usefulness) of the luggage loading area.

The MGC had only been in production for a year, however, when, in the autumn of 1968, it received a well-considered and altogether logical number of improvements. But such was the disorganisation of the new British Leyland PR operation at that time that the news was never fed to the press, and a diligent search of the motoring magazines of the period has produced no mention of the changes. It was also typical of British Leyland that the MGC GT test car they loaned to *Autocar*, and whose report appeared *after* the changes had been introduced on to the production lines at Abingdon, should have been in the original 1968-model-year specification.

The last 1968-model-year car was built at Chassis No 4235, after which the build-up of 1969-model-year cars began. I will not, however, confuse the reader any more than necessary by quoting a series of dates for the change-over for, although there was a clean break in terms of Chassis Numbers, there was something of an untidy situation at Abingdon in October/November 1968 when the last of the 1968 models were going down the tracks, intermingled with the first of the 1969-model cars!

The first 1969-model-year Chassis Number was an MGC GT, No 4236, which was finished off on 19 December 1968, and was followed by 29 further GTs. The first of the 1969-model Tourers was Chassis Number 4266, but this was finished off on 23 October 1968—two months earlier, and while the British Earls Court Motor Show was still open for business. I *said* this was a confusing period. (Incidentally, this change-over point is not made any more understandable by the GT and Tourer numbers being mixed up in some pages of the official BMC Service Parts Lists, and not in others. Those quoted above, however, are guaranteed correct, for I have double-checked the factory Chassis Book records at BL to make sure.)

The changes introduced for the 1969 models were principally as follows:

Revised final-drive ratios for manual and overdrive models
Standardisation of closer-ratio gearbox cluster for all types
Adoption of five-stud Rostyle wheels as an Export-only option
Dunlop SP68 radial ply tyres fitted instead of SP41s
Reclining front seats standardised, all types.

The reasoning behind the final-drive ratio changes had already been made clear earlier in this chapter. As a result, manual and overdrive models were both treated to lower overall gearing, which helped to give more spritely acceleration. The 3.7:1 ratio of the 1969-model overdrive-equipped car was that already specified for MGBs with automatic transmission.

The optional Rostyle wheels, which were of pressed steel, and were conventionally fixed by the normal wheel studs, but which looked rather like expensive and exclusive Italian-style castings,

For North American MGCs, it was necessary to meet the new safety regulations with this unique facia, which featured a fat padded crash roll ahead of the passenger. This car, in fact, was an MGB, as it lacks the stitched-leather steering-wheel rim (*Michael Cook*)

were enjoying something of a vogue among British manufacturers. According to official BMC literature, these wheels were made optional on 1969 models for export only; none were ever spotted on British-market cars, and the author has never seen an MGC fitted with them, even in North America. The existing choice of steel disc or centre-lock wire-spoke wheels (painted or chromed) continued, and seems to have been made by just about every buyer. (Similarly-styled wheels, incidentally, were standardised on MGBs from the start of the 1970 model-year, but these were entirely different, for they had 14in diameter rims, and four-stud fixings to the MGB's Lockheed brake drums and discs.)

At the same time, the Dunlop SP41 radial ply tyre was dropped, in favour of the SP68 radial. This was not a very significant change, in fact, as the tyre section, and its behaviour, were the same as before, but there had been some changes to the carcase and the detail of the tread pattern itself.

The last, and arguably the most necessary, change was that semi-reclining seats were standardised for the 1969-model-year cars, to counter criticism that a car of such a price, and such a specification, ought to have reclining seats in any case. It allowed the driving position to become more versatile than ever, and made the MGC a more attractive proposition. Headrests, incidentally, were optional.

During the 1969 model-year, no other important changes were phased in, and the last MGC of all—Chassis No 9102, a Primrose North American specification Coupe—was finished off on 18 September 1969 in much the same condition as that ushered in in the autumn of 1968.

⑧

The MGC in Production –
1967 to 1969

The first important point to note about the life and times of the MGC is that preparations to start building body shells were completed long before BMC could start supplying 'off-tools' engines and transmissions. It must be admitted, of course, that the Pressed Steel Co. Ltd started from the basis of the MGB body shell, which was already in volume production, but, as already explained, the changes made to accommodate the new engine and front suspension were considerable.

The result was that Pressed Steel, at their Swindon factory, were not only ready to start supplying body/chassis units before the end of 1966, but they could also find the time to supply six very special lightweight shells to the Competitions Department as well (see Chapter 9). Consequently, BMC took the opportunity to complete a short 'pre-production' run of MGCs towards the end of 1966, not only to prove that everything fitted everything else (one can never be sure . . .), but to allow representative cars to be made available to Development, Sales and Advertising departments before proper quantity production commenced. In the case of the MGC, there was also the need to pre-qualify for legislative approval in North America, where the first serious impact of the exhaust emission limitation laws was about to take place.

Assembly of the first six pre-production MGCs, therefore, began on 3 November 1966—eleven months before the car was publicly launched—but the build was a leisurely business, for the first of the batch to be completed was delayed until 25 November. The six cars in question, incidentally, were Chassis Numbers 101, 102, 104, 108, 109, and 112.

Even though the MGC was publicly launched on 18 October 1967—the opening day of the Earls Court Motor Show—it was still not properly in quantity production at this time, the reason being that BMC were only just ready to start building the engines and gearboxes. (It is worth noting, too, that the Austin 3-litre, announced on the same day as the MGC, and using the same basic engine/gearbox combination, was even further delayed, with quantity production not truly getting under way until July/August 1968.) The result was that, although the first road tests appeared in November 1967, only 230 cars were completed before the end of the year, of which a mere 41 were GTs, and of which a mere four cars (three Tourers and a single GT) were destined for North America. Thereafter, production got under way in earnest, with more than 100 cars being built at Abingdon every week.

MG's (and BMC's) battle to build up the reputation of the six-cylinder MGC not only depended on the reports published in the responsible sections of the press, and on the ability to deliver, but on the price at which the car could be sold. In Britain, there were three obvious rivals, one of which (the Austin-Healey 3000) was due to go out of production very shortly. For interest I now quote the prices existing at the time the MGC went on sale:

Model	Basic UK Price	Total UK Price (including Purchase Tax)
MGC Tourer	£895	£1,102
MGC GT	£1,015	£1,249
Austin-Healey 3000 Mk III	£915	£1,126
Reliant Scimitar GT (*not* GTE)	£1,232	£1,516
Triumph TR5 PI	£985	£1,212

In fact, the MGC was in a rarefied sector of the sports car market, at least as far as Great Britain was concerned. Most sports cars had smaller engines, Ford had still not announced their Capris, Reliant were not yet ready with the GTE hatchback, and the 4.2-litre Jaguar E-Type was in a different performance and price category altogether.

The situation in the United States, where it was hoped that most MGC sales would be achieved, was rather different, for not only was the Triumph TR series cheaper rather than more expensive as in Britain, but there was the serious problem posed by the Chevrolet Corvette. In 1969, for instance, by which time the MGC was freely available, East Coast FOB prices were as follows:

MGC Tourer	$3,395
Triumph TR6 Carb.	$3,275
Chevrolet Corvette—from	$4,438

From which it is obvious that the Corvette might have been $1,000 more costly, but that it also offered a lot more performance, and the possibility of very cheap and routine servicing arrangements.

The first blow which befell the MGC, however, was a simple and very basic one—that the press simply did not like it. The phrase 'crucified by the press' has been used in other books mentioning the model, as has that of 'character assassination'. Although I know that MGC enthusiasts are, by now, thoroughly unhappy about the way this period of the MGC's career has repeatedly been dissected in some detail, I owe it to posterity to analyse what the fuss was all about, and whether or not it was justified.

BMC, at least, did a good job of making MGCs available to most of the British motoring writers immediately after the 1967 Earls Court Show, and since several different teams, writing about several different cars, all came to the same conclusion, we may assume that there was no question of peculiar cars being issued for test, nor of any particular tester, or magazine, being afflicted by bias. Almost every historian describing the MGC's initial reception has been able to pinpoint the main functional areas of complaint—which centred on its handling, its steering, and the character of its engine—but none has ever mentioned (nor, indeed, had the knowledge of what was involved, because they were writing at second hand) another factor, which was a bitter and general disaffection toward the entire BMC group. As I was intimately involved in the working of the motoring press in 1967, when the MGC was launched, I feel that I can confirm that the MGC was not only black-balled by its own behaviour, but by BMC's overall reputation at the time.

The situation was as follows. BMC's engineering reputation had been steadily and inexorably eroding since the early 1960s, firstly as the front-wheel-drive 1800s proved to be such stodgy machines, secondly as their 'badge-engineering' escapades became more and more cynical, and thirdly as their lack of expertise in launching new cars became more and more obvious. It was in this period that it became very difficult to hold a sensible and logical

116

conversation with BMC public relations staff, so defensive had they become, and it was also a period in which you could almost guarantee that the release of a new model would be followed by several months when it was simply not available for sale. The situation became so serious in 1967 that Sir George Harriman, then chairman of BMC, attracted that eminent broadcaster, Raymond Baxter, away from the BBC to become BMC's Director of Motoring Publicity.

In 1967, however, and prior to the launch of the MGC, things did not improve, for the continued postponement of the Austin Maxi became something of a sick joke, as did the non-availability of the promised 1,275cc. engine in the front-drive ADO 16 (1100-type) saloons. The launch of the ADO 61 Austin 3-litre, although professionally carried out by Raymond Baxter at Longbridge, was something of a fiasco, not only because almost everyone thought it an ugly beast when they first clapped eyes on it, but also because it immediately became clear that here was another car which BMC had announced and which was not yet ready to be put on sale.

Small wonder, therefore, that the press were ready to be unhappy about the MGC, and BMC's attitude to its launch did not help. Although *Autocar* and *Motor* both had their usual early, privileged, look at the car, and managed to prepare cutaway drawings (a Tourer, in each case), the most prestigious sporting weekly, *Autosport*, carried no more than an un-illustrated paragraph about the car in its Motor Show number. In truth, the MGC received something of a muddled launch, or even a non-launch according to some people. One very distinguished motoring writer now a doyen in the field, looked scathingly at the MGC on display at Earls Court and commented: 'I know BMC are bloody hopeless, but you'd think they might get it right for a sports car, at least!'

Almost everything, therefore, went wrong for the MGC before it reached the public: it was not the car which MG staff once hoped it would be, it had to battle to take over the reputation of the Big Healey, and it had to survive the incompetence of its launch. Small wonder, therefore, that it received something of a drubbing from every press man who tried it.

None of them complained about the straight line performance (except to point out that its maximum speed was not as high as that of the obsolete Big Healey, its acceleration not as lively, and

This low-angle shot shows off the bulgy bonnet profile of the MGC to perfection. This is an early 1968-model MGC GT of the original press fleet

its fuel consumption rather worse), but they had plenty to say about the engine, and the handling. It was not that the engine was not powerful, and incapable of providing the MGC with good performance (for this was demonstrably untrue), but for its character. There were several ways of describing its 'feel', but it was probably Michael Bowler (Editor of *Thoroughbred & Classic Cars*), writing with ten years of hindsight in 1977, who put it best of all:

> When the 'C' arrived for road test I drove it once around the block and was appalled at the total decharacterisation . . . The engine was dead flat up to 4,500 rpm when one hoped that some power might come in, but it was actually a signal to select a higher gear. . .

It is only fair to balance Bowler's comments by reminding ourselves that as a result of making these remarks he was loaned an MGC GT—a ten-year-old example—for six months' regular use in 1978 and 1979, and that he subsequently changed his tune considerably. Among his regular comments, published in the magazine, were that:

> ...the truth is that I like the car... The GT is a very practical sports car and is quite nice looking; with its stiffer rear springs the C GT handles better. The C engine has some virtues too; it is very quiet and is remarkably smooth and torquey at the bottom end for relaxed top gear motoring.....I find the performance far more acceptable now than I did ten years ago ...

He also used the car to go to and from the Le Mans 24-hour race, and commented afterwards:

> The route had been a mixture of really good straight roads and twistier narrower minor ones, but the car kept up an effortless and smooth progress over it all, so that by the end of the trip I rate the C GT considerably higher than I did before. The handling balance is perfectly acceptable if you aren't on the screaming limit and it is an infinitely more practical road car than any Healey. Its gutless engine is the only drawback ...

The moral of this story, surely is that one should never be ready to rely on instant impressions, but to give a car's character time to emerge.

Clearly the engine had a very heavy flywheel, and compared with the Big Healey it certainly had less low-speed and mid-range torque—a feeling picked up by every tester of the new model. I also suspect that the internal power losses due to extra bearing friction and crankcase 'windage' were higher than expected by BMC. It also seems to be inescapably true that the standard engines had rather less power than that claimed for them. How else could one explain the fact that the Downton-tuned University Motors cars, with a Stage 2 conversion, went so very much quicker, but were claimed to have only 149bhp compared with the 'official' 145bhp of the standard product?

There was broad agreement as to the capabilities of the engine (John Bolster, in *Autosport*, pointed out that: 'The old Healey six was extremely rough and the extra bearings have made an almost miraculous improvement', which may have been taking the comparison beyond its normal limits), and *Autocar* probably encapsulated everything by stating that: 'The engine is something of an enigma. It is smooth and flexible, but completely lacking in sporting characteristics ... there is very little low speed torque *and* the

119

Detail of the nose of the MGC: the wide bonnet bulge was needed to clear the front-mounted MGC radiator (a component shared with the Austin 3-litre), and the streamlined blip half-way back along that bulge was to clear the dashpot of the forward of the two SU carburettors (*BL*)

engine seems reluctant to rev or develop much top end power.' Everyone seemed to agree that it felt sluggish and that the fan was very noisy.

Yet, for all that, and even with the original high gearing, the MGC was a *very fast* car. With the single exception of the Austin-Healey 3000 Mk III of 1964–7, the MGC was the fastest road car so far built at Abingdon. When Abingdon finally closed down in 1980, the MGC's title as the fastest MG had only been surpassed by the MGB GT V8, which is the third of the three cars surveyed in detail in this book. Far too often, in looking at the MGC, rather partial observers have failed to note just how quick the MGC was in absolute terms, and I take pleasure in putting them right. On main roads—on fast main roads, that is—an MGC was as rapid as almost every other British car.

Its pace across country, however, depended on the way it was asked to handle, for there was no doubt that every standard MGC was a consistent and persistent understeerer. My analysis of its layout, detailed in the previous chapter, makes clear why this should be so. No amount of special pleading by MGC enthusiasts can negate this, as all the road tests came to the same conclusions.

Extracts from tests already mentioned are conclusive. *Autocar* said that 'there is strong understeer which makes the front end slow to respond . . . it is better suited to *Routes Nationales* than mountain *cols* . . .' (that was the demonstrator registered KOV 259F), while *Motor* minimised their comments on the understeer with the remark that their car (NJB 649F) suffered more from the steering as they thought that 'Under most circumstances, therefore, the car remains a mild understeerer . . .' John Bolster, in *Autosport*, tried to be as nice as possible (as he usually is!) by stating that 'It has a pronounced understeering characteristic, which suits the rather low geared steering.' However, there was then the cautionary statement that 'It is the kind of car that can be driven very fast over a road one knows well, but the understeer rather discourages one from chancing an unknown corner at an optimistic speed . . .' (Bolster's car was KOV 259F—he drove it after *Autocar* had completed their work.)

No-one had a good word to say about the steering, and there is no point in detailing comment, for all thought it heavy at low speeds, too low geared, and that the steering wheel itself was too large. At the same time, however, there was general agreement that the straight-line stability was truly excellent, and that cruising speeds of more than 100mph were not only restful because of the high gearing, but predictable because of the well-bred stability.

All in all, testers' conclusions can be summed up by *Autocar's* now notorious final sentence from their MGC test of 16 November 1967: 'The MGC is the latest example from a very famous factory which has regularly produced classic sports cars in the past; somewhere in the large BMC complex it has lost the "Abingdon touch"' And that was really a more significant remark than might, at first, appear. It was precisely because the MGAs had been so very good, and because the four-cylinder MGB was such an outstanding mass-produced sports car, that the MGC came in for some criticism, as it was *slightly* below a really superlative standard.

One fascinating investigation into the MGC's handling was carried out by a private owner, Nicholas Brimblecombe, who took his car to the School of Automotive Studies at Cranfield, near

Apart from the slightly increased ground clearance, the only way to identify an MGC GT from an MGB GT at the rear was by reading the hatchback badge very carefully. Even in this case, only the 'C' part of the display was different (*BL*)

Bedford, where it was compared with an MGB on the inertia test rig which Cranfield possessed. The conclusions reached by the testers at Cranfield were not only that the MGC was more nose-heavy than the MGB (we all knew this already) but that the MGC's centre of gravity was 14 per cent higher off the ground than that of the MGB, and that its inertia in transverse yaw was 22 per cent higher. In layman's terms, this confirmed that MGC was 22 per cent more reluctant to change direction when being urged round a corner.

The increase in transverse yaw could only be countered by a drastic decrease in the weight of the car at each end (in other words, to reduce the 'dumb-bell effect'), and that this could be successful was proved by the performance of the very special MGC GTS competition cars built up at Abingdon by the Competitions Department in 1967 and 1968. Incidentally, Michael Bowler has also pointed out that the increased height of the centre of gravity also automatically increases the roll couple, which leads to a larger weight transfer to the outside wheels on corners, and which therefore helps to increase the under-steering tendencies. The only way to counter this, Bowler thought, was to fit an anti-roll bar *at the rear*, which is precisely what was done on the 'works' racing MGCs, with great success. (Stiffening the front anti-roll bar would not have worked, for obvious reasons.)

Once true volume production had been established at Abingdon, however, and once the shipping 'pipeline' to North America had been filled up, the MGC began to sell steadily, if unspectacularly. It soon became clear, as expected, that sales to North America were going to be much higher than those to other export markets. Compared with the MGB, however, the MGC proved to be much more popular in Britain than in North America at first. It was not until 1969 that North American sales began to outstrip those registered in Britain. It soon became obvious, too, that the

A late-model (1969-registration) MGC GT, as tested by *Autocar* as a used car in 1971, a car which proved to be considerably faster than their original road-test cars. The extra lamps, of course, and the rear-view mirrors, were not standard fitments (*Autocar*)

demand for an automatic transmission version of the MGC was quite limited—the call-up being in the order of 14 per cent—but this should be measured against the fact that there was no greater demand for such transmissions among British saloon cars of the day. Three out of every four orders for MGC Automatics, incidentally, came from abroad, mostly from North America.

In the meantime, BMC had merged with Leyland, and the British Leyland Motor Corporation had come into being. This merger, proposed in January 1968, and formalised in May of that year, had no immediate effect on the MGC (except that BMC hurried the Austin 3-litre into production to convince Leyland that they were an efficient concern—and this might have had an effect on engine and gearbox supplies if demand for either car had rocketed), nor on the changes being planned for the start-up of 1969-model-year cars. There was the long-term worry, however, caused by the wholesale import of Triumph-orientated management to BMC, and by the implications of the launch of the vee-8 engined Stag GT model. When the BMC-Leyland merger was made public, the Stag project centred around a 2.5-litre vee-8 engine, which was bad enough, but by 1969 it had been decided to use a 3-litre version of that engine. In general performance and intentions, therefore—if not in its styling or its approach to the market—the Stag was a bit too much like the MGC to be comfortable.

After a total of 4,235 1968-model MGCs had been built—the split being almost exactly 50–50 Tourer-to-GT types—there was a clean change-over on the production lines to the 1969-model-year cars. These, as already described in the previous chapter, had revised overall gearing to give better acceleration, a manual gearbox with commonised internal ratios, and were given reclining seats to improve the overall appeal of the model. By this time the basic price of both derivatives had risen by £30 (the total had gone up by more than £80 because there had also been an increase in British purchase tax), the Reliant Scimitar GTE hatchback had been launched, the arrival of the 2+2 seater Ford Capri (with a 3-litre engine option) was thought to be imminent, and it still thought that the Triumph Stag might be announced before the end of 1969.

For all that, the 1969 MGC was a rather better car than it originally had been, and made a good start, but the lasting tragedy of it all was that British Leyland never seemed to make any attempt to tell the world about this. No suitable advertising campaign was ever mounted, no special cars were raced in Britain where they might have proved a point, and no 1969-model cars were ever let out for testing by the technical press.

That they were better seemed to be proved conclusively as late as September 1971, when *Autocar* carried out a Used Car Test on an MGC GT (overdrive model) which was clearly one of the last ever made, for it had been registered on 15 August 1969. Although this car had already had three owners, and had covered more than 25,000 miles from new, *Autocar* testers discovered that it was not only more economical than their original car supplied by BMC, but that it was significantly faster accelerating through the gears, and quite remarkably faster in direct top gear itself. As an example, the time taken to accelerate from 30 to 100mph in direct top gear, without making a gear change, had been reduced from more than 40 seconds to just less than 30 seconds. Some of this improvement, clearly, was due to the lower overall gearing, but some was presumably due to the fact that the engines had gently but definitely been improved while the MGC was in production.

A greater irony, which sums up the inept BMC attitude to public relations, as far as the MGC was concerned, was that one comment in this Used Car Test was to the effect that: 'No significant modifications were introduced during the production run. ...'—and these words were written after having driven the significantly changed 1969 model!

In the meantime, the MGC had gained its most valuable publicity of all, because an MGC Roadster had been delivered to HRH Prince Charles, who was offically to become the Prince of Wales in 1969, while the car was still in his possession. Registered SGY 776F, the car is no longer owned by Prince Charles but still lives in London, with its 'keeper's address' located in the Royal Mews!

Another distinguished owner, too, was Sir George Harriman, who took over an MGC GT almost as soon as the car was launched. Sir George, of course, could have had the pick of the BMC fleet, including the use of E-Type Jaguars (for BMC had merged with Jaguar in 1966), so his choice of an MGC GT was very significant. The registration number of the car, incidentally, is no longer on record.

During 1969, however, it became clear that sales of the MGC

were certainly not on the increase, and among the ominous signs was the fact that cars began to be built for stock rather than against orders, and that the new car storage compounds at Abingdon began to fill up rapidly. Although MGB sales were booming ahead, and although the MGC was selling relatively well in North America, demand in Britain (particularly of open Tourers) was falling away. There was also the fact that the exhaust emission regulations were to be tightened up significantly in North America for the 1970 model year, and it was not going to be a simple process to make sure that the Type 29GA 2,912cc engine could be made to comply.

British Leyland, in their wisdom, therefore decided to abandon the MGC project. Officially no comment was ever made—the car was simply withdrawn from the price lists—though unofficially it was suggested that this was just one of various rationalisation moves planned by the new British Leyland whizz-kids to make their business more efficient. It was also suggested by some spokesmen that the MGC had never been a profit-maker because it had never sold in the quantities originally expected of it, and it was also made clear that the cost of the complication of carrying on with it in North America, in the face of burgeoning legislation, was simply not considered worthwhile.

Perhaps all these reasons were true, and perhaps there was no one single factor which killed off the MGC. Whatever the reasons were, the last few MGCs started down the production lines at Abingdon on 4 August 1969, though due to shortages and the necessary rectification of some details the last car of all was not completed until 18 September 1969. The last Tourer was a home market car with Chassis No 9099, and the last GT was destined for North America, and was Ch No 9102. It was one of those irritating little quirks of mass-production life that according to the Chassis Numbers a total of 9,002 MGCs *should have* been built, but that in fact there were 8,999. The breakdown of derivatives supplied by MG in November 1980, just as the Production Control department was closing down, was:

Model	Home	Export	Export USA	Total
MGC Tourer	1,403	656	2,483	4,542
MGC GT	2,034	650	1,773	4,457
TOTAL	3,437	1,306	4,256	8,999

One of the McGlen collection of MGCs is this University Motors Special GT, which included the slatted radiator grille, the under-bumper air-dam, the black-painted bonnet bulge, and the centre-lock J. A. Pearce cast-alloy wheels in its as-built specification (*Pearl McGlen*)

Of this total, the breakdown of cars supplied with automatic transmission was: home market, 335 cars; export market, 947 cars; total, 1,282.

As I have already mentioned, even after production of MGCs had ceased, there was still a significant stock of unsold MGCs at Abingdon. The last cars destined for export did not leave Abingdon until March 1970—six months after production had ended.

What happened to the home-market stock forms an interesting appendix to the life of the MGC, and is described below. The unwanted 1969 models became some of the most desirable MGCs ever built.

Note: University Motors and the Downton connection

Even while the MGC was still in production, University Motors Ltd, one of London's principal MG dealerships, were forging an alliance with Downton Engineering Works Ltd, one which

The mark of a true Stage 3 Downton engine tune on the MGC is the triple SU carburettors, mounted at a slight downdraught angle, and—for those who know where to look—there is a Downton serial number stamped on the modified cylinder head casting (*Pearl McGlen*)

effectively extended the 'production' life of the MGC for at least another year, and which resulted in some very special cars being produced. I refer, of course, to the 'University Motors Specials', a few of which were very fast indeed.

This story really began in the autumn of 1967, just after the release of the MGC (but quite unconnected with that launch). BMC (as they still were, for the merger with Leyland was yet to come) announced that a series of Stage 1 tuning conversions, by Downton, would be available from November on their Austin-Morris front-wheel-drive cars, and that the full BMC guarantee would still apply. University Motors took this a stage further when, in July 1969, they announced that they had been appointed as main agents by Downton, and that they would henceforth be fitting Downton conversions to all BMC models, and especially to MGs. This, however, was a prelude to what happened next.

As already made clear, assembly of the last MGCs began in mid-July 1969, and the last of all were completed towards the end of August or beginning of September. What only became clear some time later was that a considerable number of MGCs had

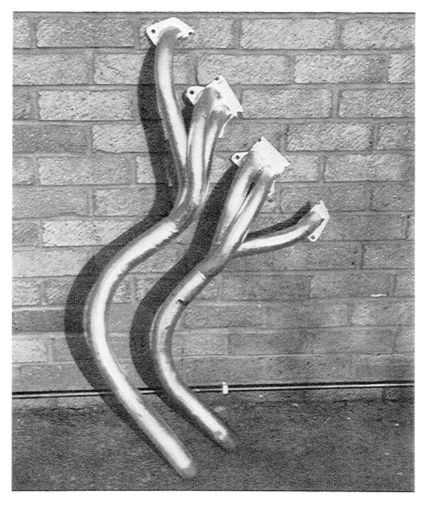

The tubular six-branch exhaust manifolds fitted to Stage 2 and Stage 3 Downton-modified MGC engine (*Pearl McGlen*)

been built in 1969 which *had not been specifically ordered by a dealer*, and that when production ceased many of these cars were still standing around at Abingdon waiting to find a good home. University Motors, having discovered the situation, then made an offer to MG for the remaining stocks and—between September and November 1969 in a series of separate operations—eventually took delivery of all of them.

How many cars were involved? Unfortunately, that is still a little uncertain. Peter Beadle, of University Motors, told Pearl and

Derek McGlen that there was a total of 176. However, a search through the record of MGC deliveries now held by BL Heritage has thrown up a slightly different figure. The search concentrated on the MGCs delivered to University Motors *after* production of the MGC stopped. On that basis, it seems to be clear that University Motors took over 118 GTs (the vast majority of which had overdrive transmission), and just 23 Tourers. That adds up to 141—and none of these cars, incidentally, had automatic transmission.

That this was a quite exceptionally large purchase is proved by a look back to July and August 1969. In July UM took delivery of ten MGCs—six tourers and four GTs—while in August they accepted six cars, three of each. However, even totting up this purchase to the 'bulk buy' only produces a figure of 156 cars, which is 20 less than that quoted from University Motors themselves. I am quite prepared to accept the difference as being due to cars which UM already had in stock, or to other MGCs which they might have taken in from other MG dealers.

Quite obviously, too, some of the 'bulk buy' cars had been in stock at Abingdon for some considerable time. The oldest Chassis Number in the list is 6002, which was completed in March 1969—and not actually delivered to UM until the end of November 1969. Many more had been built in the first half of the year.

Having taken over the cars—most of which, at least 80 per cent, were GTs—University Motors then began marketing them as 'University Motors MG Specials', to give them their full and official title. Although a variety of Downton performance tuning kits were offered (kits, incidentally, which Downton had developed for general sale and not specifically for University Motors), the majority of the cars were only treated to special paint jobs, to some degree of interior re-trimming or decoration, or to other cosmetic changes. One really important change, made to some of the cars, was that a special slatted grille was specified—a grille with alloy slats, quite unlike any other MGB/C derivative, but retaining the original chrome surround. Suspension changes were also made to some cars, to cut down on the understeer which had caused criticism from the motoring press. Indeed, it would be true to say, as other MGC experts have pointed out in previous years, that no two University Motors MG Specials were exactly alike. At least one MGC GT was substantially modified to include two more spacious rear seats, but this involved considerable modification to the floor pan and 'chassis' details, including the removal of the batteries to a position in the boot on each side of the loading area.

By 1968, Daniel Richmond of Downton had already developed three different 'stages' of engine modification for the MGC, which were already being marketed before the link with University Motors was made. Indeed, John Bolster of *Autosport* published a test of a Stage 2 Downton MGC tourer in November 1968, and I wonder how significant it is that Bolster's performance figures and those claimed by Downton were exactly the same? Might we assume that the redoubtable Bolster did not bother to take his own separate figures, and trusted those claimed by Downton?

Even though three different tuning stages were offered, with an attractive spread of prices— in 1969 the total cost of completing a Stage 2 conversion was about £160—and with University Motors' own warranty, the demand was very limited. Peter Beadle has said that University Motors carried out engine conversions on only 21 of the 176 UM Specials actually sold, so it is really quite remarkable that many of those 21 cars still survive.

Stage 1, it seems, was very rarely fitted to an MGC, and made little difference to the performance. Stage 2—also known as 'Touring Conversion No 43' by Downton—included a modified cylinder head, porting and valves, modified, polished and reprofiled inlet manifolds, two separate tubular exhaust manifolds, and a dual exhaust system to match; the claimed maximum power output was 149bhp (nett) at 5,500rpm. Stage 3—'Triple Carburettor Conversion No 45' in Downton terms—added to the features of Stage 2 by providing a triple SU carburettor installation, and resulted in a claimed maximum power output of 174bhp at 5,500rpm.

Here, of course, there are more questions raised than answers to meet them. How could it be, for example, that 'Touring Conversion No 43'—Stage 2 in UM Special language—resulted in only a marginal increase in maximum power (149 Downton bhp compared with 145 BMC bhp), yet produced considerably more performance? And how could the triple SU conversion produce 174bhp when the camshaft of the standard engine was not even changed?

While understanding that BMC and Downton might have measured their peak power figures by slightly different methods (this is something which has often happened, and can only be stopped if every power curve is measured according to strict DIN methods), I have to say that this confirms what I have always thought—that BMC's own claims for the MGC engine in standard form were over-optimistic.

It also has to be said that, while the Downton conversions made the MGC engine a much more flexible, smooth and powerful unit, they still did nothing about the engine's reluctance to speed up quickly. This failing could not only have been solved by lightening the flywheel, something which might not only have been expensive, but which might have made the car less easy to drive in heavy traffic.

The engine, as such, was capable of producing quite remarkable power outputs, as the performance of the lightweight MGC GTs prepared by Abingdon in 1967 and 1968 showed. With the help of different camshaft profiles, triple dual-choke Weber carburettors, light-alloy cylinder blocks and heads, and the Downtonising of gas-flow characteristics, a race-prepared MGC engine could produce up to 210bhp. The story of the racing MGCs is told in more detail in the next chapter.

⑨
MGCs in Racing – 1967 to 1969

Even though the BMC Competitions Department at Abingdon only ever built up racing MGCs, and even though these cars appeared in only four events spread over a period of two years, their exploits, and their specifications, are known to almost every MG enthusiast. To build up such a reputation after such limited exposure, a car needs a great deal of character—and the light-weight MGC GTs certainly had masses of that.

The 'works' MGC story began in 1966, when the Competitions Department was still managed by Stuart Turner. Although Turner had become something of a legend for his rallying strategy, he was a shrewd operator on the racing scene as well. MGBs had been raced and rallied with notable success since the start of 1963, but had never remotely been competitive against more specialised machinery. It was already known that the six-cylinder MGC was on the way so, helped along by the experience gained in racing Austin-Healey 3000s, it was decided to develop very special versions of the new car.

The first decisions were the major ones. Even if MGCs were tuned up to the standard which could already be achieved by the Austin-Healey 3000s, they would probably not be fast enough in homologated Grand Touring form to be likely to win outright, so it was decided that they should be rather specialized prototypes which just happened to look like MGCs, and which used much of that car's running gear. Accordingly, it was possible to plan for a radically lightened car with many non-standard fittings. Quite a lot of new design work was required, so the project was given the Abingdon code of EX241. It was only after the car had raced at Sebring that it was given the title of MGC GTS, where S stood for 'Sebring', as it did when the similar Austin-Healey 100S was conceived with the same object.

With the prospect of more than 200bhp being available from

race-tuned 3-litre engines, and with a matching increase in the torque capability, the body shells would have to be very stiff to provide an adequate platform to withstand twist, and to optimise the roadholding. Since one consequence of substituting light-alloy panels in place of steel panels is that strength as well as weight is reduced, there was really no possibility of using the new cars in open form, and for that reason it was decided to build up the racing prototypes on the basis of the GT structure. (As far as is known, the use of a non-standard body shape was never seriously considered, as this would have been self-defeating for publicity purposes.)

Work on this project began so early that it was possible to produce the body shells well before the MGC was even announced to the public. As we saw in the previous chapter, Pressed Steel, at Swindon, had completed the body tooling by the autumn of 1966, and once they had delivered the small pre-production batch of shells they were able to turn to the Competitions Department's requirements. Six lightweight MGC GT body shells, therefore, were built at Swindon after the pre-production cars had been produced, but before series production of bodies began in the summer of 1967.

To reduce the weight, while retaining as much beam and tor-sional strength as possible, it was decided to make the entire floor pans and stress-carrying members in pressed steel, as normal, but to have all the skin panels and much of the superstructure built in light-alloy panelling. That was very simple to say, but not at all easy to achieve in practice. Producing pressed light-alloy panels from dies designed for pressed steel is a real headache, as clear-ances have to be re-adjusted, and the likelihood of the soft alloy sheeting becoming torn at points of heavy stress (or deep 'draw') has to be expected. That, and the difficulty of welding alloy sheet to pressed steel sheet, made the building of six special body/chassis units a major undertaking. Also before the bodies could begin to be built up into complete cars, the front and rear wheel arches had to be given substantial flares to give clearance over the larger-section wheels and tyres planned for use on these cars. All six bodies were completed, and put in store, by the spring of 1967, though they could not be used as 'prototype' MGCs until after the car was launched.

The basic suspension layout of the MGC longitudinal front

torsion bars, and half-elliptic leaf springs at the rear—was retained, but with many detailed differences and improvements. Naturally the spring rates and damper settings were revised, with the settings of all dampers being adjustable. The height setting of the torsion bars could be adjusted from inside the car, through access holes in the floor pan. At the rear, there was an anti-roll bar to balance the handling and reduce the understeer, while axle location radius arms (which operated in a similar manner to those fitted to Austin-Healey 3000s) were also added.

Four-wheel Girling disc brakes replaced the front disc/rear drum set-up of the production MGC (and drew, incidentally, on the experience gained with such installations in the 'works' Austin-Healey 3000s), while there were light-alloy Minilite wheels distinguished by the use of centre-lock fixings with conventional knock-on spinners. Racing tyres were fitted, of course, BMC being contracted to Dunlop for these supplies. The other major 'chassis' modifications included the use of a much larger (24 Imperial gallon) fuel tank, and a full safety roll cage was built in to the cars on assembly. Other visual details, apart from the flared wheel arches, which made a GTS instantly recognisable from an homologated MGB GT or MGC GT, was that the cars always ran without front or rear bumpers, and their fuel tanks were fed through an enormous snap-on filler mounted high on the rear quarter, over the wheel arch on the right hand side of the car; road cars, of course, had filler caps located on the body rear closing panel, alongside the rear number plate.

The first appearance of one of these cars was in something of a disguise, for in the Targa Florio road race of May 1967 BMC entered a 'prototype' MGB GT, which was the first of the GTS cars fitted with an oversize (2,004cc) racing MGB engine. *Autosport* described it as being 'similar to the Sebring car' (which had been a steel-bodied MGB GT) 'except for SUs instead of Weber carbs, and had an aluminium body with very sexy curves and fairings', while *Autocar* got it all wrong by calling it a lightweight MGB GT as raced at Sebring. *Motor* merely called it a 'lightweight MGB GT'. Clearly none of the reporters were encouraged to poke around under the skin, for if they had they would surely have noticed that torsion bar front suspension was in use, allied to telescopic dampers, a layout quite alien to anything ever used on normal MGB GTs!

The second and last of the very special Abingdon-built MGC GTS racing models, ready to compete in the 84hr Marathon de la Route of 1968, having been 'shaken-down' at Silverstone. The flared wheel arches, the unique fuel-filler position, and the centre-lock light-alloy wheels are all obvious recognition points (BL)

Wilson McComb's authoritative marque history of MG tells us that this car finished ninth in the Targa Florio, when driven by Paddy Hopkirk and Timo Makinen, but this is quite untrue as that position was taken by Ted Worswick's Austin-Healey 3000! The truth of the matter is that the prototype GTS had a very troubled event, for Philip Turner of *Motor*, who was an eye-witness to the race, reported that it made several long pit stops which dropped it down to the tail of the field. It is true that it finished third in the Group 6 (prototype) over 2-litre class behind two eight-cylinder Porsches, one of which won the race outright, but it was not even closely in contention.

Quite clearly, however, the problems had nothing to do with the handling and stability of the car, and most of the chassis features were well-proven and ready to accept a lot more power when it became available. Although features like the wide-rim Minilite wheels were noticed by the press, they all seemed to miss (or be persuaded to ignore, who knows?) the fact that the 'chassis' was so very different, and the fact that the car was not badged as an MGB GT. Most of the usual badging was present, but the 'B' part of the title was deliberately missed off when the car was being decorated. As the car was really neither an MGB nor an MGC, the logical decision was made—to badge it as an MG GT.

Having had one rather undistinguished outing, this car, registered MBL 546E, was put back in store at Abingdon, where the Competitions Department chose to wait for the MGC production car to be unveiled; the personnel there were not only concentrating on the very successful Mini-Cooper S rally programme, but also on the development of the front-wheel-drive BMC 1800 saloons for rough road work. It was not until March 1968—ten months after the original Targa Florio outing—that the same car re-appeared (it was still the only car to be completed), this time being described as a prototype MGC for its entry in the Sebring 12-hour Race of that year, and being fitted with race-modified six-cylinder engine and transmission.

Superficially the engine of the racing MGC looked somewhat like that of the normal MGC, except that an aluminum cylinder head was used and, of course, there were three dual-choke Weber carburettors and a full-flow racing exhaust manifold instead of the ordinary breathing arrangements. In this form, with a cast-iron cylinder block, and with a 0.040in enlarged cylinder bore, a

One of the MGC GTS models under preparation for the 1968 Marathon de La Route. This particular car is obviously brand new, which means that it was the second example, eventually registered RMO 699F. Note the turret-mounting for the rear dampers (*BL*)

2,968cc MGC racing unit could produce at least 200bhp at 6,000rpm. It is worth recalling that a light-alloy cylinder head had first been used on a BMC competition car (a Big Healey record car) in the 1950s, and that a light-alloy head for the Austin-Healey 3000 was homologated for use from the beginning of 1962. However, as already made clear in an earlier chapter, the MGC engine differed in almost every major way from that fitted to Austin-Healey 3000s, so there was no question of the Big Healey's racing engine being used in the MGCs.

At this point, I ought to divert from the chronological story and mention the experiment engines which not only had an aluminium cylinder head but an aluminium cylinder block as well. This was done not only to take even more weight out of the car (the head itself was worth more than 20lb, while the light-alloy block must

A *real* bonnetful of engine, three dual-choke Weber carburettors and all, of one of the very rare MGC GTS racing models. The large converted plastic container mounted on the scuttle is actually an oil-catch tank! (*BL*)

All race-prepared MGC GTS engines were rare, but those having light-alloy cylinder blocks were rarer still—which makes this picture of an engine/transmission assembly at Abingdon a real collector's piece (*BL*)

have put the saving up to more than 60lb), but also to allow even greater and quicker dissipation of heat from the super-tuned racing engine itself. Harking back once again, the first all-alloy BMC straight six was the prototype C-Series unit seen in the Austin-Healey 3000 which had been prepared as a Group 6 'prototype' for the 1967 RAC International Rally.

Three experimental all-alloy racing engines were also built on the basis of the new and redesigned MGC engine, but were not fitted at first. Memories fade, and all records have been lost, but it now seems certain that such a light-alloy engine was certainly used in the second MGC GTS to be completed and in the 1968 Marathon de La Route, as I have official BMC pictures taken of the preparation of that car with the all-aluminium engine standing alongside waiting to be craned in to the structure. One such engine, at least, was sold off, and is now in a privately-assembled GTS.

Attention to detail by mechanics in the Abingdon Competitions Department is evident in this shot of a brand-new MGC GTS cockpit being prepared. The 'Identity' switch to the right of the fuel gauge was actuated to switch on the light positioned on the roof above and behind the driver's seat (*BL*)

At Sebring, the only GTS still to exist was driven by Paddy Hopkirk and Andrew Hedges, and put up a stirring performance around the rough airfield circuit. It had a trouble-free run, handled and behaved superbly, and finished tenth overall out of the 69 starters. Not only that, but it finished third in the entire Prototype category, behind the Porsche 907 eight-cylinder racing prototypes of Hermann-Siffert and Elford-Neerpasch, which also just happened to finish the race in first and second positions overall. Apart from the very hot Chevrolet Corvettes and Mustangs, the MGC was the only production-based car to get into the top finishers, and it must have given the team a real confidence boost. The 3-litre class win was an extra!

In 1968, however, the team did not take a lightweight car to the Targa Florio in Sicily (they took a steel-bodied MGB GT instead), but concentrated on preparing two GTS models for the Marathon de la Route event at the Nurburgring in West Germany. This was an event which had grown, rather unhappily, out of the Spa-

Sofia–Liège marathon rally, which had been hounded off the roads after the 1964 event. The rules and regulations surrounding the event were far too complex to describe here, but basically it involved an 84-hour non-stop race around the combined 17.6 miles of the 'North' and 'South' Nurburgring road circuits. Complicated penalties were applied for over-long pit stops (this, in fact, was to affect the chances of one GTS rather severely), routine service was only allowed for 20 minutes every 1,300 miles (74 laps, in fact), and any car not completing a lap in under 25 minutes was automatically excluded—that being equivalent to 42.2mph. To succeed at this event not only required a strong and fast car and determined and durable drivers, but also a great deal of luck, a very organised pit crew, and a team manager with the mind of a computer, and with cunning to match. In 1966 BMC's team entry had been managed by Peter Browning (who became Competitions Manager in 1967 when Stuart Turner moved on), when an outright win by an MGB was recorded, and in 1967 a Mini-Cooper S finished second overall to a works-entered Porsche 911S. It all augured well for 1968.

The first appearance of an MGC GTS was actually with a 2-litre four-cylinder engine installed. Paddy Hopkirk and Timo Makinen drove MBL 546E in the 1967 Targa Florio, some months before the MGC was publically revealed. Note that the 'C' part of the hatchback badging has been deleted (*Autocar*)

MBL 546E, the original MGC GTS, at the Nurburgring in the 1968 Marathon de la Route—an event in which it finished sixth overall in spite of all manner of dramas with the braking system (*BL*)

Two MGC GTS lightweights were prepared, MBL 546E having been brought back from the Sebring 12-hour race and re-prepared for Julien Vernaeve, Andrew Hedges and Tony Fall to drive, while the new car was was registered RMO 699F, and entrusted to Roger Enever, Alec Poole and Clive Baker. (In 1966, incidentally, the winning MGB had been handled by Andrew Hedges and Julien Vernaeve, while Hedges, Vernaeve and Tony Fall had all been in the second-placed Mini-Cooper S in 1967, so the portents were good, as the experience of the drivers was of the highest possible quality). There was a very strong entry of 60 cars including 'works' Lancias and Porsches; the GTS cars were likely to be as fast as any but the best Porsche 911s.

84 hours of racing! That's more than three whole days of driving, almost non-stop, with the car, the drivers, the mechanics, and the team management all getting progressively more tired. As a race to watch, for the spectators, it could be extremely boring, but to anyone who was closely involved, and who could understand

the mathematics involved and the various permutations which could be applied, it was a fascinating exercise in four-dimensional motor sport—the fourth dimension, of course, being that of time.

There was a massed start at 01.00 hr on the Wednesday, and by daybreak the field was beginning to settle down, with one of the Porsche 911s being hotly pursued by the older of the two GTS cars (MBL 546E), then a Lancia Fulvia HF, and with the other MGC hovering around fourth place. However, in the early hours of Thursday, when well over 24 hours and 2,000 miles of racing had been completed, the newer car (the Enever-Poole-Baker example, fitted with the all-alloy engine) retired with engine overheating, having expelled all its cooling water—an effect symptomatic of a blown cylinder head gasket.

The Vernaeve-Hedges-Fall car, MBL 546E, carried on serenely and by the Friday morning it was lying third behind the leading Porsche 911s, and catching them up at the rate of 30 seconds per 13-minute (82mph average) lap. Later that day, however, the car made an unexpected pit stop with failing brakes, caused because the front pads had completely worn out; at a previous routine service it had been decided not to change the pads, which looked good for a further 75 laps, but which inexplicably wore out before that time.

What happened next is an amazing tribute to the stability of the MGC GTS, the bravery of the driver, and the resourcefulness of the BMC team management. I can do no better than quote *Autocar*'s Stuart Bladon, verbatim from the race report:

> Fall took over the wheel and sat patiently in the car while mechanics hammered and bashed to try to remove brake pads which had distorted and almost welded into position. Eventually the left ones were forced out with not a scrap of friction material left . . . Still they fought with the right one, losing one (penalty) lap every minute, and then had to abandon it and change the whole caliper assembly. The 20 minute limit for exclusion was nearing, so Fall was sent off to do a lap completely brakeless . . . After *averaging* nearly 60mph with no brakes, Fall was back after 18 minutes, but although he came in slowly he could not stop. Team manager Peter Browning was dragged along by the car, and it simply bounced over a chock thrown under the wheels. Only when Fall managed to get into reverse did it stop, and it had then well and truly overshot its pit. Knowing the rules, which expressly forbid any car to go backwards on the track, Browning sent him round again.

This time Fall lapped in an incredible 16 mintues. His classic remark afterwards was: 'It gets a bit exciting at times', and he added that he

One of the two works-entered MGC GTS cars at speed in the 1968 Marathon de la Route. The car is actually landing after a hump (note the rounded profile of the rear tyres) and is much higher off the ground than it would normally be (*BL*)

was 'glad no one got in the way while I was doing 125mph along the back straight.'

They made sure of stopping him this time, and it took a further eight minutes to bleed the system and restore efficient braking. With the earlier stop the total 25 lap penalty dropped the MG from third place—only a lap behind the leader—to eighth.

After that, there was nothing more to be done than to plug away for a strong finish. Before the event finished on the Saturday, 84 hours after it had started, the GTS had clawed its way up to sixth place, and finished a net total of 28 laps behind the winning Porsches. The victory which had once looked to be in sight had been snatched away from BMC—but without the experience of the team they might have been excluded altogether.

This event, however, was the last in which an MG motor car was officially entered by the Abingdon-based factory team. By the autumn of 1968, the first effects of the formation of British Leyland were already being felt. Rumours that the Competitions Department was to close down were unfounded but, as Peter Browning has pointed out in his book, *The Works Minis*:

> ... the programme of activities was to be drastically reduced to events in those countries where our winning· could give the company both marketing and publicity benefits. Lord Stokes had put the emphasis on winning. ... He had also expressed a significant dislike of rallies. .

For 1969, therefore, this policy resulted in rallying activities being cut back, in most of the money being spent on a Mini racing programme, and in the MGB/MGC racing programme being cancelled altogether. There was only one more chance for the MGC GTS models to be raced, at the 1969 Sebring 12-hour Race, where both cars were entered by the BMC North American importers, the Hambro Corporation, in company with an MGB GT. MBL 546E was driven by two Canadians, Bill Brack and Craig Hill, while the newer car, RMO 699F, was driven by Paddy Hopkirk and Andrew Hedges.

The older car ran into considerable trouble, and eventually limped to the finish at the tail of the field, but the Hopkirk-Hedges GTS was driven very rapidly throughout, only making routine stops for tyres and fuel, and eventually finished very strongly in fifteenth place. Clearly the two British drivers relished the handling of their big cars, for *Motor*'s reporter said that: 'according to one observer the car was being driven "as if there were no tomorrow" '. There was no question, on this occasion, of the GTS taking a class victory, as it was a Group 6 car of more than 2-litres, and that class was won by the Chris Amon/Mario Andretti Ferrari 312P prototype which was second overall in the event.

The two factory-built racing cars were then sold off by Hambros in North America, officially being 'exported' in May 1969, though they had not, in fact, ever returned to Britain from the Sebring race. The newer of the two cars (RMO 699F) has since disappeared from view, and is thought to have been broken up, but the original car—MBL 546E, the one with the more distinguished record as a competition car—returned to Britain in the 1970s, and at the last count was to be found on display at the Cheddar Motor Museum in Somerset.

The other four lightweight body/chassis units were then sold off to John Chatham, a motor trader specialising in BMC sports

The last semi-official appearance by an MGC GTS was in the Sebring 12 Hour Race of March 1969, when Paddy Hopkirk and Andrew Hedges (who is at the wheel in this shot) took the car to 15th place overall (*Autocar*)

cars who had already made his name in British sports car racing with an ex-works Austin-Healey 3000. In the next year or so, Chatham built up one car for his own racing use, built up another as a road car for British Leyland Motor Sport press officer Alan Zafer to use, completed a much-modified version for Modsports racing in Britain, and finally built up the last example as a road car and sold it to a private owner.

The first car, registered VHY 5H—which is a Bristol number— was finished in time for Chatham to use it in the 1970 Targa Florio, but it was not at all suitable for this twisting course in Sicily. In addition, its American specification tyres were not right, the engine was misfiring, and there was even a small fire during a pit stop to add to the owner's misery.

Both the road-going cars, incidentally, are still in existence, and may be identified by their flared wheel arches and their Bristol registration numbers—the Zafer car was VHW 330H and the 1971 car, owned by W. H. Gardner, was EHW 441K.

What was such a disappointment about the short and rather disjointed competition career of the lightweight MGCs was that British MGC owners never had a chance to see them in action. Although neither factory-built car ever achieved a major success (but what a 'so-near-so-far' instance the 84-hour Marathon experience was!), all their drivers agreed that they were remarkably nimble, fast, strong, and versatile. If only BMC had stayed independent of Leyland, and if only the GTS programme could have been pursued more seriously, we might have seen all manner of improvements to the MGC road car. If only . . .

Preserving the MGC Today

Over the years, several new cars have got themselves a bad reputation at first, have fought themselves up to respectability, and
have been retired in a much more favourable light. The MGC was
absolutely typical of this. Although there were some people (often
very uninformed, or even biased, people—some of whom, to my
certain knowledge, never even drove an MGC) who did not like
the car, evidently there were thousands who did. After all, a
production rate of nearly 9,000 cars in less than two years is one
which would have made some of MG's rivals rather proud; it was
only the British Leyland accountants, hidden many light-years
away from the showrooms, who thought the MGC not worthy of
their attention.

Nowadays, more than a decade after the last MGC was built,
the car has a steady following, and a growing reputation. People
owning MGCs, or looking to buy such a car, consider the car on
its merits, and have no false hopes for it. They know it is a big car,
a relatively heavy car, and above all a fast car for main road
motoring. In its environment it provides a beguiling combination
of high speed at low cost. What is fascinating to me, too, as a
historian, is that MGC enthusiasts seem to be more vocal about
their cars than MGB GT V8 owners do about theirs; further, you
rarely find one type of owner admitting to the advantages of the
other type of car. All this goes to prove that the character of the
MGC is very different from that of the V8-engined and the four-
cylinder-engined cars.

Of the 8,999 MGCs built, it seems that about 1,000 cars are still
in existence in Britain (though more are being 'discovered' all the
time, as the car's reputation, and the enthusiasm for it, increases),
which represents about a quarter of the cars originally registered.
Rather more MGCs were exported (more than 4,250 went to
North America, for instance), and though it is impossible to be

One of the impressive collections of MGCs owned by Derek and Pearl McGlen. This car was more than 10 years old when photographed, and is still in astonishingly original condition. Only the Goodyear radial-ply tyres are non-original (*Pearl McGlen*)

accurate, it is thought that more than 1,000 MGCs may still be in use in North America alone. In parts of that continent the climate is kinder to pressed steel unit construction bodies that it is in Britain—and it is the condition of the MGB/MGC body shell which governs whether or not a motor car is worth maintaining.

What *is* certain is that very few MGCs are now being broken up to provide spare parts for other and better examples. Enthusiasts seem to be willing to spend a great deal of time on the rejuvenation of an MGC, reasoning that it was almost unique by MG standards, and is worth the effort.

At this point, too, I should emphasise the fact that although the 'chassis' items at the front of the MGC—front suspension and structural items—are unique to this model, there is a useful duplication of engine and gearbox items with the ADO61 Austin 3-litre saloon. As far as MGC enthusiasts are concerned, it is good to know that there is no discernible interest in the preservation of the big Austin saloons, and this means that worn-out (or even roadworthy) examples of the car are available at real knock-down prices. Just over 10,000 Austin 3-litre models were built between 1968 and 1971, the majority of which were sold in Britain. In most respects the engines and the gearboxes were the same as those used in the MGC, as was the radiator, and there are even some internal final-drive components which are also the same. Clearly, to know exactly what is common, and what is not, you need to compare the appropriate Austin 3-litre and MGC parts manuals.

I can summarise the position regarding MGC parts supplies from BL very simply: the MGC and the Austin 3-litre have both been out of production for more than ten years, so BL (Unipart) no longer support the stocking of mechanical spare parts unique to those cars. In other words, do not expect much help from BL, or from BL dealers, in regard to the engine, the transmission, or the front suspension of the MGC.

For the same reason, you should not expect to find BL dealers interested in finding body/chassis panels for the MGC where they are special to that car. However, the rest of the body panels, external and internal, which are common with the MGB of that period, are still available, and likely to remain so for some years, even though the MGB finally dropped out of production in 1980. Since more than half-a-million four-cylinder MGBs were built between 1962 and 1980, there will clearly be a demand for parts which will remain commercially viable for BL to satisfy for years to come.

In regard to the MGC and MGC GT structures, therefore, the easy-to-find panels common with the MGB (Mk II onwards—i.e. 1968 models and later derivations) are the skin panels, with the exception of the bonnet pressing, and all the internal structural panels aft of the front seat area at lower level, together with all the scuttle and toeboard panels. If they are not *actually* common, they are very nearly so, and can be modified to suit; it is certainly worth altering slightly non-standard panels, as an alternative to not having new sheet metal at all.

Some of the special MGC body and 'chassis' panels are now being remanufactured, but by no means all of them. The bonnet panel, however, is made in steel instead of in the light alloy which was standard on production MGCs. Major underfloor members, however, are not available, so a truly badly corroded MGC must be patched up, and existing members reinforced, rather than be treated to new panels or 'chassis' members. The good news, however, is that underfloor sections of the MGC appear to be intrinsically very strong, which means that almost any surviving car forms the basis of something which is worth re-building.

Very little of the MGC's decorative identification differs from that of the MGB of the period. It follows that MGB bumpers, octagons, window surrounds, door handles, and other details are all the same, and can be used on an MGC. Even the 'C' of the MGC badging on the tail is a separate casting, and supplies of that letter are now available. At the time of writing, the bright stainless steel strip mounted across the bonnet bulge above the radiator was not available, but plans were afoot to remedy this; it was hardly a major obstacle to restoration of the car!

Glass—windscreen, door windows, hatchback windows (including the optional heated variety)—was all common with the MGB, and presents no problems, but if you are a fanatic for originality you should remember that tinted glass was never even an option on this model.

Most soft trim items—carpets, trim panels, floor coverings, seat materials—have been, or are being, remanufactured, and present no problems. In any case, they are identical with MGBs of the same period, so the demand is significant, even after all this time.

As with the MGA Twin-Cam, the major instruments of the MGC can be re-built and restored to full health, which is probably just as well, as they were not the same as those used on contemporary MGBs. The rev-counter, for instance, took account of a six-cylinder rather than a four-cylinder engine, and the calibrations were also different.

Under the car, and out of sight, are the major transmission casings—gearbox, overdrive or automatic transmission, and the back axle. In all except detail, the gearbox internals were the same as those used on the Austin 3-litre, and the wider set of ratios have, in fact, been used on MGBs built up until the end of 1980, so it should always be possible to rebuild the gearbox of an MGC from late-model MGB parts. The overdrive, however, was not common after 1974, when a different component was standardised on MGBs. The Borg Warner gearbox—the Type 35 design—was the single most popular automatic among medium-sized British cars for many years in the 1960s and 1970s. Although it was never very popular among MG customers, it found favour all over Europe in more mundane models. Apart from its own special settings and control linkages, the MGC automatic is built up from standard Borg Warner components. Borg Warner themselves, or the automatic transmission specialists which have sprung up in Britain or

North America, will be able to service this box for many years to come.

Although the MGC back axle used Girling drum brakes, whereas that of the MGB used Lockheeds, (and the axle end plates therefore differ) the two designs were the same in most respects. Apart from the difference in crown wheel and pinion ratios, many components are common, and remained in production until 1980. It follows that the rebuilding of an MGC axle should present no problems. I should repeat, however, that there is no way of knowing, from the markings on the casing, what ratio is fitted inside, and this will have to be checked out in the usual way. Three different sets of ratios were involved, and for the record, these ratios were achieved by the following combinations of teeth:

Ratio	Pinion teeth	Crown wheel teeth
3.07	14	43
3.31	13	43
3.70	10	37

I am sure I do not have to remind an MGC owner that the front suspension of this model was unique, and not shared by any other MG, BMC, or even BL car. Most of the items in this suspension are no longer available from MG dealers. However, it is now possible not only to rebush the front king-pins (which wear fairly readily, and are an obvious source of trouble if roadworthiness tests have to be passed), but to buy completely reconditioned sets of kingpins. Torsion bars rarely seem to need changing (there is no history, it seems, of heavy rusting, or of other deterioration), while new telescopic shock absorbers are still readily available from suppliers of Armstrong equipment (Armstrong were the original suppliers). If orginality is not required, alternative types like Koni or Spax shock absorbers can also be fitted.

On the question of brakes, Girling suppliers can provide any type of component (or even the complete caliper, it seems) for the MGC, and it may be worth noting that the front disc caliper is the same as that used on later model Rover 2000s. Supplies of new front discs are also available. The original discs may have become corroded rather badly; they can be skimmed down, once or even twice with care, but they should never be allowed to get too thin for arduous use. The rear drum brake—9in diameter drums, $2\frac{1}{2}$in wide shoes—is another standard Girling item, and can easily be rebuilt if required. Note that this brake is not the same as that used in the Austin 3-litre. Incidentally, it is a measure of the popularity and the versatility of the MGC's Girling brake system that the same front brake pads were specified for Rover 2000s, Triumph GT6s, and Triumph TRs built up to the end of the TR6. The rear brake shoes were also to be found on 3-litre Ford Capris, and on all the 1970s variety of Lotus Elites, Eclats and Esprits.

Many MGCs have wire wheels, and although it is usually cheaper to have loose and rattly old wheels rebuilt by specialists, it is also possible to get new wheels, either silver painted, or chrome-plated. The MGC wheel, in fact, has a 5.0in rim width and is by no means the same as that fitted to the Austin-Healey 3000, which had a different layout of spokes and a 4.5in rim width. The Austin-Healey will fit the hub of the MGC, but it is by no means as strong, and is not recommended. The same Dunlop wheel supplied to MG for use on the MGC, incidentally, was also supplied to Triumph for use on the TR5s and TR6 models of the period; spline fittings and offsets were identical, and the wheels are therefore freely interchangeable.

Which variety of MGC is now the most desirable? A few years ago the Roadster would certainly have received most people's vote, but now that the model has achieved 'classic' status it is the MGC GT which is the most popular. It now seems to be generally agreed that the GT is much the more practical machine, it is more versatile, and it also suits the character of the MGC's performance rather well. My own experience of driving both types of MGC is that the GT has the better handling balance as well.

All in all, the reputation and standing of the MGC has improved considerably in recent years, and it is certainly looked upon as a more thoroughbred machine today than ever it was in the late 1960s when still in production. But was the MGC GT (or better still, a University Motors modified MGC GT) as good, not as good, or better than, an MGB GT V8? That is the sort of question likely to provoke very long-running and passionate arguments among MG enthusiasts, and I for one would be foolish to make a definite pronouncement, one way or another. Which is as appropriate a point as any to turn my attention to the last of the 'Mighty MGs'—the MGB GT V8 of 1973-6.

⑪
MGB GT V8 – Lightweight Rover Power for the 1970s

On 17 January 1968, British Motor Holdings agreed to merge with Leyland Motors. It was a business decision which altered the whole shape of the British motor industry. In a stroke, too, it killed off any lingering thoughts MG management might have had about preserving any independence that the old BMC management had allowed them.

The immediate result, which disturbed John Thornley and his staff quite profoundly, was that MG was now to be in the same corporate group as Triumph—a marque with which they had been in direct conflict for many years. Worse—and this only came to be confirmed in the following months, as British Leyland decisions began to filter down to individual factories—was the fact that the real 'top brass' at British Leyland were now 'Triumph men', and the implications of this for MG's future were truly horrifying.

I must, at this point, include a very brief review of the way in which this merger came about. During the 1950s and the 1960s BMC (of which MG was a part) was always Britain's largest motor-car manufacturer. It had taken over the Pressed Steel body producing company in 1965, and in 1966 had merged with the Jaguar Group, thus giving rise to British Motor Holdings. In the meantime, however, Leyland Motors, the lorry manufacturers from Lancashire, had taken over Standard-Triumph in 1961, and followed this up by annexing AEC, the London-based truck and bus manufacturers, in 1962. While all this was going on, Rover had bought Alvis, and then agreed to join the growing Leyland Group in the winter of 1966/7.

The final merger, of Leyland with BMH, meant that the industry's 'Big Five' was immediately reduced to a 'Big Four'. The other three constituent members were Ford, Vauxhall and Rootes

(Chrysler), all of whom were controlled from North America, so the British Leyland combine became not only the largest but also the *only* sizeable British-owned car-making group. The formation of British Leyland, it should be admitted, had been encouraged by the British (Labour) Government, who were currently wedded to the concept that 'Big is Beautiful', and wanted to see a large and prospering export-conscious concern as something of a British flagship.

In the months which followed, many fine words were spoken, but down at factory level there were few immediate changes. Except that the corporation was now controlled by Lord Stokes, and that new-car design at Longbridge was being directed by Harry Webster, both of whom (in private-car terms) were 'Triumph men', MG carried on basically as before. During 1968 they were busy churning out as many Austin-Healey Sprites, MG Midgets and MGBs as they could, while at the same time they were trying to bring up the demand for six-cylinder-engined MGCs.

In 1968, the Corporation had several sports cars competing with each other, and more were planned. Triumph, for instance, were building Spitfires, GT6s, and TR5s, with (at that time) the vee-8 engined Stag and the TR6 due in 1969. Rover had just had the mid-engined vee-8 P6BS project cancelled by Leyland, while Jaguar were building a lot of six-cylinder E-Types and were planning to introduce a vee-12 engined car as soon as the engine itself was ready.

It was an almost impossibly complex situation which (with hindsight) British Leyland should have dealt with much more ruthlessly, and rapidly, than they did. There are grounds for suggesting that the Stag, with its entirely special engine, should never have been introduced at all, and on the other hand it is generally agreed that the productionised version of the mid-engined Rover sports Coupe should have been produced as quickly and energetically as possible. None of these things were done; indeed, one characteristic of British Leyland's formative years was that there was much talking, boasting, and posturing, but very little action.

A proper rationalisation programme (of the sort which Leonard Lord had carried out, on a rather smaller scale, with BMC in 1952/3) would have resulted in several surplus engines being abandoned, and in one outstanding design—the light-alloy Rover V8—being used in other models crying out for it. The Stag engine (so technically interesting, but so unreliable) and the MGC/Austin 3-litre six-cylinder engine (obsolescent heavyweight engineering—traditionally British) should both have been cancelled. In the event, the six-cylinder engine stayed in production until 1971, by which time the MGC had been dropped, and after which the Austin 3-litre also followed it into oblivion.

At this point, private enterprise took a hand in new-model development, where a factory was not allowed to do so. At a time when the design engineers at Abingdon were struggling (successfully, it should be emphasised) to keep ahead of the burden of new North American safety and exhaust emission legislation, an engineer from Kent, Ken Costello, shoe-horned a Rover V8 engine into the body/chassis unit of a four-cylinder MGB, with outstanding successful results. His first car was completed in 1970, and even though it was virtually never advertised, a demand for such conversions soon appeared, and the car was put into production on a hand-built basis at Farnborough, in Kent.

At this stage, I should make it quite clear, British Leyland were supplying Rover 3500 (P6B) engines, rated at 150bhp (DIN), to Costello Motor Engineering Ltd, and I have repeatedly been assured that at the time they neither knew nor appeared to care what use Costello were making of them. It was not until 1971, when building of the cars was sometimes approaching two per week, and when the conversion had taken on a neat and business-like appearance, that Costello demonstrated one of his 'Costello V8s' to British Leyland executives. Predictably, I suppose, he was told that such a conversion was not a practical proposition for quantity-production applications. That, however, was for public consumption. Privately, British Leyland were impressed, and one result (so Wilson McComb tells us in his MG history) was that the chairman, Lord Stokes, soon wanted to know why MG designers could not do the same thing, or even improve on it!

It was exactly the challenge Roy Brocklehurst, Don Hayter and their colleagues at Abingdon needed at this time. They had, after all, designed an all-independent suspension front-engined car (EX234) in 1968, which might have replaced the Midget *and* the MGB, but had seen it cancelled. And they had then designed a new mid-engined car (ADO21) in what was effectively a design

The impressive snout of *Autocar*'s MG Costello V8 road-test car, showing the non-standard 'egg-box' grille, and the sizeable bulge in the glass-fibre bonnet panel. The road wheels were similar to, but *not* the same as, those eventually fitted to Abingdon-built MGB GT V8s (*Autocar*)

competition with Triumph regarding a new mass-production sports car for the 1970s, and seen that cancelled as well. The result was that a V8-engined prototype was on the road within six weeks, and approval to refine the concept for production was speedily given.

There were, of course, many major, and detailed, differences between the 'private enterprise' Costello V8 conversions and the car which MG eventually put into production themselves, not least being the fact that Costello found it increasingly difficult to get supplies of Rover V8 engines from British Leyland to produce his cars. It has often been said that once British Leyland discovered the purpose for which they were supplying engines, they immediately refused to deliver any more to Costello, and this broadly appears to be true. The cut-off, however, was neither complete nor abrupt. The existence of the car was known in 1971, but although MG's own project got under way in the same year, Costello V8s were still being built in 1972—as witness the fact that a car was made available to *Autocar* to test in the spring of that year. There is no doubt, however, that by the time MG were ready to start building their own V8-engined cars, in the first months of 1973, the supply was finally and irrevocably cut-off. Should we really have expected anything else?

The definitive Costello V8s of the 1971/2 period used 150bhp (DIN) Rover engines in virtually unmodified form, which is to say that the 10.5:1 compression ratio pistons were retained, together with the inclined and opposed SU HIF6 Carburettors, which were high enough to make a specially-bulged glass-fibre bonnet panel essential. To match this, Costello took something of a risk by retaining the unmodified MGB all-synchromesh gearbox (whose internal ratios, let's not forget, were the same as those used in the original non-overdrive MGC), but specified a 9.5in diameter diaphragm spring clutch. The existing MGB/MGC hypoid bevel back axle and differential was quite strong enough, though the final drive ratio was raised from the 3.909:1 of the MGB to 3.07:1, as used in the 1967–8 manual transmission MGCs. Standard suspension, brakes and steering were all retained from the current MGB and, unless the customer demanded it, so were the same wheels and tyres. Most cars, however, were fitted with special sculptured light-alloy cast wheels, which looked similar to those finally adopted for the factory's MGB GT V8, but were very different. The 'Costello' wheels, in fact, were made by Dunlop and had steel rims riveted to the cast-alloy centre, these had also been made optional on Reliant Scimitar GTEs from the autumn of 1971. Apart from these wheels, where fitted, a special 'egg-box' grille, the bulging bonnet, and badging at the rear, there was no other way of recognising a 'Costello', for even a single exhaust tail-pipe was retained.

Autocar's road test of a Costello V8, incidentally, must have come as a great encouragement, not only to Ken Costello himself but to the engineers and planners at Abingdon who were already working on their own version of such a car. In their issue of 25 May 1972 (a date, incidentally, by which the specification of the

In most early Costello V8s, the 3,528cc Rover engine was fitted in standard Rover form, which is to say that it was fitted with opposed semi-downdraught SU carburettors (*Autocar*)

'official' V8-engined car had been frozen), *Autocar* testers had this to say:

> We can think of no reason why BLMC are not producing it themselves, and their product planners ought to be ashamed at not having spotted this potential market. . . . As a conversion, we rate this car as perfect, and as a model in its own right it deserves the highest praise. . . .

My consideration of the private-enterprise V8 car ends virtually at this point, though I ought to point out that it is still available to this day. Dave Vale of the V8 Conversion Co took over the design some time ago, and cars are still occasionally being produced for owners of four-cylinder MGBs who desire a complete rejuvenation of their cars. Ken Costello is now no longer connected with the business. According to Dave Vale, no historical records remain, so he can only estimate that about 200 have been built since the model was put on sale in 1970, and it seems to be fairly certain that the vast majority of these were GTs, and only a few were open

Tourers. The conversions, of course, can no longer take place with new engines. Since 1972, secondhand Rover V8, or even refurbished Buick engines, have had to be used. It is thought, incidentally, that only one six-cylinder MGC has been converted to V8 power but, as Dave Vale also supplies kits of parts to customers and does not see the end result himself, he cannot be certain.

Before leaving the Costello V8, however, I should also draw attention to its price. In 1972, when *Autocar*'s test appeared, the 'basic' car cost £2,443, and the addition of overdrive, radial-ply tyres, alloy wheels and a heated backlight boosted that price to £2,616. At the same time, the MGB GT cost £1,459, the overdrive Reliant Scimitar GTE cost £2,300, the Triumph Stag (hardtop model) £2,387—and the cheapest 3-litre Ford Capri a mere £1,538. It is against that sort of background that we have to judge the slow sale of the Costello V8, and the problem facing the quantity-production car when it was ready for launch.

Abingdon's problem, once they had been given the go-ahead, was that they had been asked to modify nothing unless it was absolutely necessary, and they also had to accept the inevitable commonisation with the existing four-cylinder MGB wherever it was necessary. This helps to explain, for sure, why the V8-engined car announced in 1973 was by no means as distinctive, and different, from the MGB as it deserved to be and as, in truth, it ought to have been.

At this moment, it is worth recalling that the four-cylinder MGB had been on sale for nine years by the time the factory's V8-conversion job got under way, and that more than a quarter of a million cars of that shape had already been delivered. In that time, mechanical improvements had been minimal, and changes to the styling had been almost entirely cosmetic; the MGB style, in fact, was already in danger of getting to look too old, and of becoming boring, old-fashioned, and unacceptable to the customers. Apart from the fact that it would soon be necessary to re-jig the basic design to take account of new United States legislation on bumper heights, and on the need for bumpers which had to withstand 5mph traffic accidents without being damaged, no major changes were proposed for the next couple of seasons.

Roy Brocklehurst and Don Hayter, therefore, were confronted with the need to develop a new and (by definition) rather more expensive high-powered MG, without being allowed to alter its styling to make it look obviously different from the existing four-cylinder car. They were also faced with the fact that the facia design, switchgear, and general layout were, by this time, beginning to look distinctly unergonomic, and not at all suitable for the type of motoring that V8 power was likely to promise.

The major surprise, to me, is that no alternative engine to the Rover light-alloy vee-8 seems to have been considered. It was true that the Rover engine's major attraction was that it was not only powerful, but also compact and light in weight, but it was also a fact that production capacity was still somewhat limited. If the 2,997cc Triumph Stag V8 engine had not been rather too heavy, it would have seemed to make as much engineering sense (design *and* production engineering) to use it as it was to use the Rover engine; the Stag unit, after all, was rated at 145bhp (DIN)—almost the same as the Rover V8—and it was only used in one model. Its production was not, by any means, at the limit of capacity, for Stag sales were hardly setting the world on fire. Another advantage, at this point, was that the Stag engine was 'de-toxed' for use in North America, while the Rover V8 engine was not.

If that was a strange decision, and likely to cause head-scratching to BL watchers for many years to come, the decision to build only closed GT derivatives of the design was not. Other sources have suggested that the open MGB body/chassis unit was not rigid enough to withstand the much-increased torque and performance of the Rover V8 engine, but I find that almost impossible to accept. On the other hand, I recall that the MGB has always been recognised as one of the most rigid open sports car shells ever put into production, and on the other I would remind technically inclined readers that the main points of stress likely to be aggravated by the torque of the V8 engine were in the rear suspension and in the drive line mountings, neither of which would be much affected by the lack of a GT roof and associated structures.

The real reason for not offering an open-top derivative of the V8-engined car was that it was rapidly becoming clear that there would only be a very limited demand for such a model, especially as the decision had been taken to sell the MGB V8 *in Great Britain only*. It was only in countries which combined a splendid climate with restrictive speed limits that open cars were still very fast sellers; the West Coast of the United States, California in particular, was an ideal example. There was no longer much real pleasure in spending a great deal of money on an open car, when it had to be closed up in poor weather, and when it was positively uncomfortable, noisy and smelly to drive it fast with the hood down. Customers for small, cheap, and less fast sports cars (like the Midget) were happy to buy open sports cars, but those for more expensive types were not. At MG, the writing on the wall had been obvious with the MGC (most of the redundant home-market stock taken over by the University Motors had been GTs, for instance), while other manufacturers had all followed the same trends. For that reason, and probably for that reason alone, British Leylands' product planners decreed that the V8-engined car should only be sold as a GT.

The question of *where* it could be sold was one settled for MG without their participation and—it has to be said—without their consent. As I have already pointed out earlier in this chapter, the true decision-makers at British Leyland in the early years were ex-Triumph managers and, even though they never admitted to this in public, it became quite clear that they always tried to give Triumph cars the best deals, the first bite at new investment and, where appropriate, the widest choice of markets. By 1972, when planning for MGB GT V8 production was almost complete, MG had already found that they were progressively having to withdraw their cars from traditional export markets (to give Triumph, and the planned TR7, a clear run), and were being forced to concentrate on the domestic and United States markets only. Worse still, the continuing burden of new legislation emanating from the United States meant that they continually had to review what cars they could sell over there. (One result, which became effective in 1974, after the MGB GT V8 had been launched, was that the GT version of the MGB body shell was withdrawn from the market; thereafter it was only available in Britain.) MGBs, therefore, were no longer being exported to the traditional 'Empire' markets, or to the continent of Europe.

It was with such crippling restrictions on their trade coming into force that MG prepared to launch the V8-engined car. Even though, at one time, it was thought that the car could perhaps be exported to North America (and seven pre-production cars to a proposed USA-spec. were actually built in the winter of 1972/3), this was abandoned when the cost of federalising the car, particularly the V8 engine, became clear. The MGB GT V8, perforce, would have to be built for sale in Britain only and, in view of the limited market for large-engined sports cars of any type, this was a real gamble to take.

A consideration of the car's technical specification follows in the next chapter, but before moving on to that it is right, also, to ask why British Leyland (not MG, you understand) thought it right to specify the use of a de-tuned Rover V8 engine. The transmission, after all, would have to withstand very little more torque if the normal engine was fitted (the actual figures were 201lb ft (DIN) for the standard Rover engine, and 193lb ft (DIN) for the engine eventually specified—a reduction of a mere 4 per cent), and there was no physical reason why it should not fit, nor practical reason why Rover should not build it.

Real reasons, as the reader will have divined by now, are (or were, at least) almost impossible to extract from British Leyland staff responsible for this turbulent period, but in the case of the MGB GT V8 the real reason for the use of a de-tuned engine was almost certainly so that the car would not be embarrassingly quick by comparison with other cars in the group like the Triumph TR6, and the Stag. It was the Stag, in fact, on which so much investment was currently riding, which was already gaining something of a poor reliability reputation and not performing in quite the way that its specification suggested it should. *Autocar*'s best Stag figures, published in June 1971, just before work on the MGB GT V8 began at Abingdon, showed a maximum speed of 116mph, a standing start quarter mile in 17.1 seconds, 0–60mph acceleration in 9.3 seconds, and overall fuel consumption of 20.7mpg. Right from the start, it became clear that a V8-engined MGB could beat all those figures by a considerable margin if the 150bhp Rover car engine was installed; with a lower state of tune there was still an improvement in favour of the MGB GT V8, but it was not quite as embarrassing at it might have been.

Once MG had been given the go-ahead to put the V8-engined car on to the British market, they pushed on as rapidly as possible, and it would have been nice to have had it ready for display at Earls Court in the autumn of 1972. The times, and the complexity of motor cars, had changed, however, and it was no longer possible to move from prototype to production car in 15 months, as had been achieved with the MGA in 1954-5. The best that could be expected was for production cars to become available within two years of the first car being started, and the staff at Abingdon went ahead on that basis. If they were lucky, the MGB GT V8 would be on sale in the spring of 1973; if not, its launch would have to be delayed until the middle of the summer.

Abingdon had done its best within a very restricting design brief. Now it was all up to the sales force—and to the customer.

⑫
MGB GT V8
– The Technical Analysis

It will already have become clear, from the previous chapter, that as far as Abingdon's production planners were concerned the MGB GT V8 was a much easier car to build than the MGC had been. The V8's engineering was much more closely based on that of the four-cylinder MGB than the six-cylinder MGC had ever been. It meant that, even though the V8 was never built and sold in the same numbers as the MGC, it must have been a more profitable proposition. In particular, the pressing and assembly of body shells by Pressed Steel Fisher at Swindon must have been very straightforward.

Before analysing the engineering layout, and the attractions, of the MGB GT V8, therefore, I ought to review the many features and components which were shared with the current-model four-cylinder MGB. This study, at least, shows that much common sense had gone into the detail design of the V8 car; indeed, from the start-up of 1975-model-year (black-bumper) four-cylinder MGBs, the special pressings necessary to the V8 car were incorporated in all MGB body shells.

In the first place, of course, I should remind the reader that there was no open Tourer version of the V8 car, and that every Abingdon-built V8 used the sleek fastback GT body shell. Quite a few 'Costello' or privately converted V8s have been created, but none of them originated at Abingdon. The most common reason given for the fact that no open V8 car was ever offered was that the Tourer bodyshell was not rigid enough to withstand the power and torque of the V8 engine. Frankly, I do not believe this, as the MGB body/chassis unit has always been renowned as being very rigid in all respects. BL would certainly have taken the trouble to develop an open version of the V8 car if they had seen a market for

167

it, and I am convinced that they did not do so because their product planners only forecast sufficient demand for a GT derivative. It is also worth recalling that at this time there was something of a motor industry fixation with the attractions of the Anglo-German Ford Capri, of which there was no open version, and with which Ford had already cornered an impressive slice of the market.

Throughout Europe, car makers had also discovered that the market for truly fast open cars was falling away rapidly. The vocal few who wrote complaining letters to the specialist magazines were certainly not increasing in numbers, for most customers could not live with the wind battering inevitably linked with the driving of an open sports car at more than 100 mph. To pose elegantly up and down a hot speed-restricted boulevard in Los Angeles was one thing, but to rush up and down a cold, wet and certainly smelly motorway in Britain was quite another.

A study of the specification of the MGB GT V8, therefore, must start with a brief résumé of the four-cylinder MGB GT which was being built in 1973, after which it is possible to pinpoint differences. This is much more straightforward than it was in the MGB–MGC situation, as far fewer changes were needed to the basic body shell.

1973-model-year MGBs still looked very much as they had done in 1962, in that there had not been any changes to the basic body style—to what our North American friends term the 'sheet metal'—though there had been several changes to the grille, decorative detail, and interior. Externally, the 1973-model MGB could be identified by the new radiator grille, with its chrome surround and black plastic mesh, and by the use of rubber-faced bumper overriders, while it retained the four-stud Rostyle wheels first introduced on 1970 models, and the British Leyland badge fitted to the kerb-side wing only, just ahead of the passenger's door. It had also been given a simulated leather trimmed steering wheel with silk chrome finish spokes. For the British market radial ply tyres had been standardised and (on the fastback GT) so had the heated rear window feature.

No further visual changes were planned for the 1974-model-year MGBs, but there would be new and bulkier energy-absorbing rubber overriders for North American market cars. Radial ply tyres would be standardised for all markets, along with a brake

Overhead view of the definitive MGB GT V8 engine installation, showing that the same basic plenum inlet chamber has been retained as is used on Rovers, but that a special secondary inlet manifold mounts twin SU carburettors at the rear of the engine, near the bulkhead, and that specially designed air cleaners and trunking gather their intake area from each side of the vee-8 engine (*BL*)

The MGB GT V8 engine/gearbox installation ready for fitment to the body/chassis unit. Overdrive was standard on every V8-engined car (*BL*)

servo and hazard warning flashers for the British market. The automatic transmission option, which had not been a marketing success, was about to be withdrawn.

Compared with the four-cylinder MGB of the period, very few changes were needed to the body/chassis unit to make it the basis of a V8-engined car, and most of these were connected with the installation of the bulky V8 engine itself. The shell was built in basically a home-market condition, and the major change was to raise the shell bodily one inch off the ground to rationalise on bumper heights, for legislation thought to be brewing. This entailed lowering the mounting pivot for the front end of the rear axle's half elliptic leaf spring (and fitting a suitably re-cambered spring), while the detachable front cross-member was given extra plates which effectively lifted the front of the body shell further off the front suspension, whose geometry was not altered.

There were no body shell changes under the tail, floor or centre sections of the body, nor any others connected with the exterior lines of the car itself, but several pressings changes were needed to panels surrounding the engine bay, and in the nose. The inner wheel arches, or engine bay valances, had to be reshaped to allow more space round the engine, and there were even local dimples close to the exhaust manifolds. At the same time, and to provide

170

more clearance around the large bell housing and rear of the cylinder block, the 'chassis' side members, running back over the top of the front suspension cross-member and sweeping under the toeboard to the centre cross-member under the seats, were re-shaped.

In the nose, there was a slightly different bonnet locking plat-form (across the car, ahead of the radiator)—different only in that there were extra mounting holes for the twin electric cooling fans. Also ahead of the radiator, the platform supporting the oil cooler had scallops joggled down to allow sufficient clearance for the blades of those fans. In most other respects, the front ends of the four-cylinder and V8-cylinder MGB GTs were common.

Behind the engine, the need to provide clearance for the rear of the angled cylinder heads and valve covers meant that toeboards had to be reshaped. In fact they were angled back at about four degrees towards the gearbox tunnel openings, though the lower sections of these toeboards were not in any danger of becoming fouling points, and were not changed.

In regard to external decoration, the MGB GT V8 retained the same front grille, with its black plastic mesh, but there was a different lower air scoop behind that grille (and out of sight). There was a squatly styled 'V8' badge on the grille itself, on the kerb-side wing panel ahead of the British Leyland badge, and on the hatchback on the opposite side from the MG octagon. No V8 badge was mounted on the driver's side front wing, this being put down to 'penny pinching' by MGB GT V8 enthusiasts.

The only front suspension changes were to the spring rates, and the use of non-crushable lower wishbone rubber inserts. A Lock-heed brake servo was standard, the front discs were much thicker (0.45in, compared with 0.30in for the MGB), the brake caliper was a Lockheed amalgam of Triumph 2.5 saloon inner casting and MGB outer casting, and there were different wheels and tyres.

The wheels, although looking superficially similar to those used on the Reliant Scimitar GTE of the period, were not quite the same in detail, as they had different wheel centre/rim offsets, and different rim widths. The wheel stud hole centres were indeed the same for both cars (even though the Reliant used Girling brakes), and the Reliant wheel can certainly be fitted to an MGB GT V8, but they were most emphatically not the same wheel. In detail, the cast-alloy centres were precisely the same, but the steel rims

(*Above*) The original style of 'chrome-bumper' MGB GT V8, looking almost identical with the four-cylinder-engined cars; this was modified in the autumn of 1974 to the 'black-bumper' style (*below*) used on all MGBs built from that date. Which do you prefer? (*Both BL*)

riveted to them were different in size and position. Nor were these wheels fitted to any other regular production MG model, except for the 750 'Anniversary Special' four-cylinder MGB GTs built at Abingdon in 1975, when they were painted gold.

The MGB GT V8's tyres, incidentally, were of 175–14in section, and had a high-speed HR rating, whereas the tyres fitted to four-cylinder MGBs were normally of an SR rating, with 165–14in dimensions. (The current Reliant Scimitar tyre, by the way, was 185HR14in, another difference from the MG).

The rear axle of the V8-engined car was exactly the same as that which had been standardised on all other MGBs since the summer of 1967, which is to say that it was of Salisbury-type construction. The final drive ratio was 3.07:1, the same as that which had already been used on non-overdrive MGCs built in 1967 and 1968. The brakes, the piping, and the handbrake linkage were all the same as those fitted to four-cylinder MGBs, and no extra suspension links of any type were provided. Compared with the four-cylinder MGB, only the leaf springs and the dampers were different.

It would be far too easy to suggest that the power unit of the MGB GT V8 was nothing more than a lightly modified light-alloy Rover unit, dropped in to an engine bay already prepared to receive it—and it would be quite wrong. In the past it has been suggested that the MGB GT V8 merely took the Range Rover unit, with minor alterations, but this ignores the many changes specifically made to tailor the engine to the MG installation.

In the previous chapter, I explained why it had been decided to fit the engine in its lowered-compression form, using Range Rover pistons (and a ratio of 8.25:1), but this is really the only connection with the Range Rover. Other MG experts have told me not only that there is little in common with the special fittings for the Range Rover (which even had Zenith-Stromberg carburettors whereas passenger car Rovers used SU instruments), but that most items are those used on the Rover $3\frac{1}{2}$-litre saloons and Coupes (P5Bs, in Rover parlance) which went out of production in 1973, just before the MGB GT V8 was announced.

Surprisingly, it was not necessary to design a new oil sump (to allow clearance of the MG's cross-member), the Rover item being quite satisfactory. In the parts lists, incidentally, it is easy to pick out an original and unmodified Rover part by its part number, which contains no letters, and mainly begins with the digit '6'. An example of this is in the cylinder head region, where the head casting itself is Part No 614642, whereas the special cast rocker covers (complete with an MG octagon) are BHH1208 and 1209.

The major differences are obvious. To suit the installation, the exhaust manifolds are special, as was the exhaust system. As already mentioned, cast-alloy valve gear covers used the same style as those fitted to current Rover models, but there was an MG octagon on specially produced castings for the MG application.

On the Costello-modified MGBs, which used Rover engines with Rover inlet manifolds and carburation, it had been necessary to construct a glass-fibre bonnet panel with a pronounced hump. British Leyland's policy was to retain the unmodified MGB bonnet panel, and to modify the carburation to suit. This was achieved in a most ingenious manner, by very original thinking. Since it was clear that there was insufficient space for the carburettors on top of the engine in the conventional position, it was decided to move the carburettors to where there *was* enough space, and to arrange the manifolding to suit.

The result of this was that two horizontal SU HIF6 carburettors (HIF6 indicates Horizontal Integral Float instruments with 1.75in chokes—the same choke size, but not quite the same instruments as those fitted to current-model Rover passenger cars) were positioned at the back of the engine, with a two-piece light-alloy inlet manifold connecting them to the engine. The complications, however, were not over, for there was a wide and slim air box behind the carburettors (and immediately in front of the heater box on the bulkhead), individual paper element air cleaners sitting atop the engine rocker covers, and the actual air intakes mounted above the exhaust manifolds, incorporating British Leyland's patented hot/cold air intakes. The primary inlet manifold, or plenum chamber, was a modified version of that used by Rover, but the secondary manifold (called an Adaptor Assembly by the official Parts List) was specially designed.

Because of the rather confined nature of the engine bay space, and because a more substantial radiator was needed in front of the existing body panelling, there was no space for the conventional Rover cooling fan to be employed. In its place, and ahead of the radiator, there were two electrically driven cooling fans, mounted side by side, and only in operation when the water temperature rose above a certain level.

(*Above*) The 1973-model type of MGB GT V8 and (*below*) the 1974-6 'black-bumper' variety which took its place (*Both BL*)

In addition, and also signalling the fact that the engine bay was likely to get very hot because there was very little air space for the forced draughts to circulate, an engine oil cooler was standard. This was mounted in the conventional MGB position, on a panel immediately ahead of the water cooling radiator, just ahead of the twin cooling fans.

A comparison of power outputs is interesting. Clearly, I should compare the engine fitted to the MGB GT V8 with those fitted to the Rover 3500S (P6B) saloons and to the Range Rover, but I also feel that a comparison with the obsolete MGC is instructive. These were the peak figures:

Model	Maximum Power	Maximum Torque
MGB GT V8	137bhp (DIN) at 5,000rpm	193lb ft at 2,900rpm
Rover 3500S	150bhp* (DIN) at 5,000rpm	204lb ft at 2,700rpm
Range Rover	130bhp (DIN) at 5,000rpm	185lb ft at 3,000rpm
—and the MGC—		
MGC	145bhp† (net) at 5,250rpm	170lb ft at 3,400rpm

* When the Rover 3500 was introduced in 1968, its power output was originally quoted as 161bhp (net), a figure which was changed and recalibrated more than once in the ensuing years. The manual transmission 3500S was, in fact, more powerful than the 3500 Automatic!
† The MGC power output was never quoted to the more severe DIN standard, and my estimate of 130bhp (DIN) can be no better than a good, experienced, guess.

Clearly, therefore, the MGB GT V8 was not only more powerful than the MGC had been, but it also had considerably more torque into the bargain, especially at low speeds. Allied to the fact that it was also much lighter (2,390lb for the V8, compared with 2,610lb for the MGC GT), it had a better power/weight ratio. The MGB GT V8 had a ratio of 128bhp/ton, whereas the MGC GT had a power/weight ratio of 111bhp/ton. This, of course, was mainly due to the commendably light weight of the alloy Rover engine, which was little heavier than the four-cylinder MGB engine which it displaced.

To harness the massive torque of the V8 engine, the MGB GT V8 was given yet another derivative of the all-synchromesh gearbox which had been adopted by the MGB/MGC range in the autumn of 1967, and which was still used by the MGB. I can summarise its construction by saying that it was *basically* the same as that fitted to the MGB/MGC models, but that it was considerably different in detail. Further, the MGB GT V8 was fitted with overdrive as standard, and there was no automatic transmission option (which was just about to be dropped from the MGB lists at the end of the 1973 model-year).

The gearbox, therefore, followed the same basic design of the MGB/MGC box, which is to say that its shaft centres, shafts and many of its components were the same as those to be found on the MGB, along with the complex selector arrangements and the remote control gearchange. However, to match the box to the Rover V8 engine, and to encompass the 9.5in diaphragm spring (Borg and Beck) clutch, there was an entirely unique main gearbox casing/bell housing cover.

Yet again, however, a new set of internal ratios were specified— the third different set so far specified for this gearbox family in MG cars (and not forgetting different ratios specified for the Sherpa van which also used the same basic casing and gearbox for a *very* different application) and one which was not to be used on any other British Leyland model. The complications and convolutions of the MGC installation have already been detailed in Chapter 7, but here, for comparison, are the internal ratios of the MGB of the period, and of the new V8-engined car:

Model	Internal ratios
MGB GT V8	1.00, 1.259, 1.974, 3.138, reverse 2.819:1
MGB 4-cyl	1.00, 1.382, 2.167, 3.44, reverse 3.095:1

A study of the original information published by British Leyland shows that only the constant mesh gear wheels in the boxes were different; the company had obviously gone to very little trouble to optimise the ratios.

Unlike the MGB, and unlike the obsolete MGC, the Laycock overdrive fitting was standard. However, there is a typical bit of BL confusion as to what gears it operates on. According to the original press information of August 1973, and the road test cars issued at the time, overdrive was only operable on top gear. I am assured, however, by MGB GT V8 owners, that early cars were equipped with overdrive operation on top *and* third gears. The change to top-gear-only operation took place at gearbox No 1404, which was *approximately* the same Chassis Number but not exactly the same due to the way in which engines, gearboxes and body/ chassis units were mated together at Abingdon. As far as the

The facia/instrument panel of the MGB GT V8 of 1973, almost identical with that fitted to current-model four-cylinder cars (*BL*)

gearbox ratio was concerned, the overdrive converted top gear from a direct drive ratio of 1.00:1 to 0.82:1, raising the top gear mph/1,000rpm figures from 23.4 to 28.5.

The other significant difference between the MGB GT V8 and the home market four-cylinder MGB of the period was that the V8-engined car had US-type market steering column switch gear (the overdrive switch was on the left side—ie, the gear-lever side—of the column), and as this required a larger column shroud it automatically meant that the main speedometer and rev-counter instruments had to be reduced in size, and of course they had different calibrations.

Like the four-cylinder-engined car, semi-reclining front seats

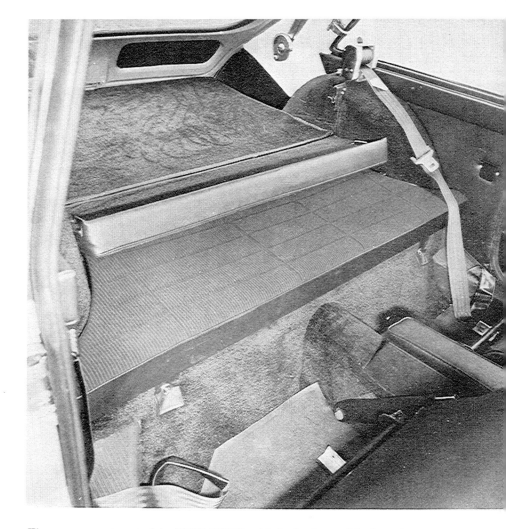

The rear compartment of the MGB GT V8, with the backrest of the 'occasional' rear seat folded down to increase the rear loading space

were standardised, as were the adjustable headrests, and like every MG GT there was the provision of tiny, but still useful, '+2' rear seating. In all important respects, however, the interior trim, furnishing, and general appointments of the MGB GT V8 were the same as those of the ordinary MGB—and this, in the writer's opinion, might have been one reason for the way in which MG found the car rather hard to sell. No matter from what angle the car was viewed, it was almost impossible to tell, from a casual glance, that here was something rather special with a big and very powerful engine. The MGB GT V8, in other words, was much too much like the MGB for its own good.

Between the spring of 1973 and the summer of 1974, very few

MGB GT V8s were equipped with 140mph speedometers, and had their rev-counters amber-lined at 5,200rpm. Note, too, that the oil-pressure calibrations were very low—the Rover engine was designed to operate all the time at between 35psi and 40psi (*BL*)

changes were made to the MGB GT V8, apart from minor de-velopment alterations, and some rationalisation of bumper over-riders and a change to the rear number plate lamp positions.

Let us now turn to the 'black-bumper' cars of the 1975 and 1976 model years. In the autumn of 1974, every MGB and MGB-derived car, irrespective of the market for which it was intended, was given a major facelift to bring it in line with a new set of United States legislative requirements. Basically this entailed lift-ing the four-cylinder car bodyshells an inch higher off the ground to accord with the standard already established on the V8 cars, and the fitting of vast and controversially styled deformable '5mph' bumpers to the front and rear. It was, however, a much more major change than it looked.

As far as the MGB GT V8 was concerned, the start-up of 'black-bumper' production (in October 1974) did not involve any important change to the mechanical equipment of the car, except that the engine oil cooler was now mounted below (rather than above) a body panel leading back from the front end to the base of the water-cooling radiator. No changes were made to the height of the car, nor to suspension settings, engine power, or gearing.

The bumpers themselves were of flexible black polyurethane, backed by suitable reinforcements to make them soft, yielding and able to revert to their original shape after a low-speed traffic accident. That much was perfectly acceptable—at least, it was if the regulations demanded it. What infuriated many MGB enthusiasts was that the new bumpers were also big—very big, *and* very heavy. At the front the assembly was styled into the downward sweep, incorporated its own radiator air intake, and meant that anything approaching a traditional MG radiator grille had to be abandoned completely, while at the rear the bumper curved away under the tail, and swept along the back of each rear wing to give a modicum of protection to the tail lamps. At the same time, a decorative 'GT' flash was incorporated at the top of the metal panel on each side of the car between the rear quarter window and the hatchback aperture, to cover an unleaded body joint!

Several important body sheet metal changes were made to accord with the new bumpers. At the front, the main 'chassis' rails had to be changed, there were significant differences to the front wing panels, to the front panels, and to the cooling ducts which are normally out of sight. At the rear, there were changes to the fore-and-aft structural members, the rear wings had different lower cut-outs to match up to the new bumpers, and the rear and lower skirt panels were all modified. It would not, in fact, have been possible to carry on making 'chrome bumper' and 'rubber bumper' cars without a great deal of added expense and aggravation—both at Pressed Steel Fisher at Swindon, and at Abingdon.

MGB GT V8s with this revised body style, however, were not modified any more, and the last of all was built in the autumn of 1976, about $3\frac{1}{2}$ years after the first production car had been assembled. The life and times of the car, however, are described in the next chapter.

⑬

The Fastest-ever MG in Production – 1973 to 1976

The first road tests of the 'private-enterprise' Costello V8 had appeared in 1972, and there had been speculation about an 'official' MG version for some time, but it was not until the middle of August 1973 that the MGB GT V8 was officially revealed. At the time it came as a great surprise (a pleasant one, it must be said) to the motoring press to realise that a new BL car had not only been launched, but was ready for sale, for in recent years the corporation had built up quite a reputation for announcing a car before they were ready to deliver any to customers. The Triumph Stag and the Range Rover were cases in point.

Although the first true 'production' V8 car, Chassis Number 114, was built towards the end of March 1973, more than a dozen pre-production cars had been assembled at Abingdon before this. The very first car, Ch No 101, had been run down one of the four-cylinder MGB lines in December 1972, actually being finished on 12 December, and the next dozen were all started by the end of January 1973. Some of those original cars were for engineering purposes, or for use in the satisfying of legislative requirements, but seven of them were left-hand-drive models, with North American specification features, but with non-Federalised engines. These cars—Chassis Numbers 101, 102, 104, 105, 108, 109 and 110—were really 'samples' to see if the North American market was interested, and if it was worth carrying out an extensive ratification programme on the V8 engine. As it happened, the proposal to send cars to North America—or indeed to build left-hand-drive cars at all—was abandoned, and the seven vehicles were re-sold to customers in Europe. No other left-hand-drive V8s were ever built, so we can state with certainty that every *series-production* MGB GT V8 was a right-hand-drive car.

In marketing terms, it would have been desirable to launch the V8 at the peak buying time for British customers, which is, traditionally, May and June, but BL were determined to have stocks of the V8 to sell *before* they revealed the car, and delayed the launch until August. By this time more than 400 examples were already in the dealer pipe-line, and production was going ahead at the rate of about 40 cars a week.

The motoring press seemed to like the car—for its spirited performance, and its ingenious mechanical packaging—but they were not at all happy about its unchanged interior styling, or about its high price. The headlines over the technical analyses were quirky, as might be expected. *Autocar* asked the question 'Look what's gone into the MGB GT?', and sub-headed this 'Superb Rover V8 in "B"—at last'. *Motor* were more succinct, and expected readers to know what it was all about; all they had to say in the headline was 'B Sting'.

There was, of course, the problem of the price. Loaded up with features all optional on the four-cylinder car, like overdrive, tinted glass, heated rear window—and, of course, the V8 engine—the MGB GT V8 cost £1,925 (basic), or £2,294 with special Car Tax and VAT. *Autocar* compared it with its opposition, and in their road test commented:

> To hope to sell well against this powerful competition, the MGB GT V8 has to rely heavily on its excellent smooth power unit, for in most respects of appointment and comfort, it does not score over the opposition ... It is difficult to understand how a £500 differential can be justified between the MGB GT V8 and an MGB GT with the 4-cylinder engine and the same optional equipment.

Apart from the ageing aspect of the styling and behaviour (the basic MGB design had, after all, been on sale for nearly eleven years when the V8 car was launched), the price was a real problem. I have taken the trouble to look up the competition of the day—cars with similar performance aspirations, and/or body treatment—and the results presented in Table 13.1 in descending order of total price are interesting.

These, of course, were only the prices which applied at the time the car was announced. Britain was entering a period of very high inflation (at one point, prices in general were going up at the rate of more than 30 per cent a year), and the MGB GT V8, along

Table 13.1   *Prices of MGB GT V8 and comparable cars, 1973*

· Model	Total British Price (Including Taxes)	Body type
Datsun 240Z Coupe	£2,535	2-seater hatchback, no open version available
Triumph Stag Hardtop	£2,533	2 + 2-seater, no hatchback. Open version also available
Reliant Scimitar GTE (o/d)	£2,480	2 + 2-seater hatchback, no open version available
TVR 3000M Coupe	£2,464	2-seater, no hatchback, no open version
MGB GT V8	£2,294	2 + 2-seater hatchback, no open version available
Morgan Plus 8	£1,967	2-seater open sports, no hardtop version
Ford Capri 3000GXL	£1,824	2 + 2-seater coupe, no hatchback, no open version
Ford Capri 3000GT	£1,651	2 + 2-seater coupe, no hatchback, no open version
Triumph TR6PI	£1,605	2-seater open sports, hard-top available

with its rivals, was subject to price increases totalling 169 per cent in the three years of its production life.

The placing of the MGB GT V8's price at such a level was something which puzzled me at the time, and one which has never properly been explained. Perhaps some strange accounting procedure, related to BL's inter-divisional costs, to the forecast rate of production, or even to the market aspirations of the car itself, explains it, but BL themselves never tried to justify it. The problem was not that the MGB GT V8 was almost as expensive as the long-established Reliant Scimitar GTE, or as the more bulky Stag, but that it was very much more expensive than Ford's 3-litre Capri.

Not only was the V8 39 per cent more expensive than the existing Capri 3000GT, but BL's planners must surely have known that a re-designed Capri was due for launch early in 1974, with much sleeker lines, more interior space, and a hatchback body. If they did not, then the motoring press most certainly did. I do not believe I am over-emphasising the competition from Ford for, as far as Britain's sporting motorists were concerned, the Capri was *the* standard-bearer in the category. It had been launched in

1969, had been improved persistently in the following three years, and had rapidly established its reputation for giving high performance at low cost.

Annual 3-litre Capri sales in Britain gave a target for MG to aim at. In 1970 5,290 had been sold, and the next three years fluctuated at around the 3,500-a-year mark. Clearly the market for this sort of car was fairly restricted anyway; even so, the sales of Reliant Scimitars, Triumph Stags, and TVR 3000Ms were completely overshadowed by the Capri, and it looked as if the 1974 Mk II car would be even more successful. The fact that Ford had previously established no thoroughbred sporting pedigree did not seem to matter.

It was in the face of this sort of competition that the £2,294 MGB GT V8, £747 more expensive than the four-cylinder MGB GT without extras, went on sale in August 1973. No one at MG doubted that it was a good car, nor that it would be a great success, although they had to wait to see what technical writers thought about it, remembering how most of these people had crucified the MGC way back in 1967.

Autocar's test car was HOH 920L and was well liked, though the question of price was emphasised. The test's sub-heading was 'MG elegance, Rover smoothness', which just about summed up what most people thought about the car. Not only did the drivers love the performance—a standing quarter-mile time of 16.4 seconds, and a maximum speed of 124mph were very rapid indeed by current standards—but they were impressed by the high gearing, the refinement and silky smoothness of the Rover-manufactured 3,528cc engine, and by the overall fuel economy recorded, which came within a fraction of beating that of the last four-cylinder MGB GT they had tried, in 1971. They did, however, have this to say:

> Such shortcomings as excessive wind noise, a harsh ride and heavy steering may be forgiven in an out-and-out sports car, but they have no place in a GT car costing over £2,000. More unfortunate still is the fact that such shortcomings are accentuated by the superb smoothness and relative quietness of the excellent Rover V8 engine . . .

Motor, Britain's other authoritative weekly magazine, said the same things in their own way, and their initial summary included the comments: 'For—smooth flexible engine, well-chosen gear ratios and overdrive . . . Against—poor low-speed ride, dated decor, high wind noise at speed . . .' In the text, however, there is the very significant comment that: 'Initial impressions are always illuminating, and among *Motor*'s often cynical staff the reaction was quite enthusiastic . . .' On the deficit side, however, they described the price as 'hefty', the dashboard as 'rather crude and austere', and the ride as 'almost unacceptable'. Their test car, incidentally, was registered HOH 933L, and it was slightly quicker than *Autocar*'s example, with a standing quarter-mile time of 15.8 seconds, and a top speed of 125mph, but the overall fuel consumption was rather heavier, at 19.8mpg.

In the meantime, Philip Turner of *Motor* had interviewed Leslie Lambourne, general manager at Abingdon when the MGB GT V8 was launched, and had drawn some interesting information from him, including the following:

> [The MGB GT V8] . . . will however only be sold on the home market, for the supply of Rover V8 engines is not sufficient to enable the new model to be exported in large numbers. The fear is that if only a small quantity is shipped to the United States, then the result could well be many cancelled orders for the B by potential owners hoping to obtain one of the scarce V8s. . . . If, however, the reception in Britain for the new V8 is so favourable that the production of V8 engines has, in any case, to be expanded to meet demand, then eventually the new car may be sold overseas as well.

All of which was fine and logical as far as MG, and BL, were concerned, and it would still have been very tidy for a historian to accept if only it had been the truth. It was not that MG (and BL) were actually telling tall stories about engine supplies, but that they did not truly know how their new model was going to sell, and wanted to have a believable 'party line' ready in case it did not.

It is time, therefore, to knock the myth of limited availability of Rover-manufactured V8 engines on the head, once and for all, and this can easily be done by quoting a few production statistics which BL have since made available. The situation was that the Rover V8 had gone into production in 1967, first for the big Rover P5B $3\frac{1}{2}$-litre saloons, next for the P6B 3500 models, and after that for the four-wheel-drive Range Rover. The last of the P5B saloons— the big and ponderous 'Great Auntie' $3\frac{1}{2}$-litre saloons—had been built in May 1973, just as series production of MGB GT V8s was getting under way. The only other user of Rover V8 engines in 1973—about five units a week—was Morgan, for the Plus 8 sports car.

The statement that there was not enough Rover V8 engine capacity to keep MG adequately supplied simply does not stand up to close examination, and the accusation that it was an engine shortage which caused the car to be withdrawn from production in 1976 is quite literally not true. In 1973, Range Rovers were being built at the rate of about 150 cars a week, and V8-engined Rover private cars were being built at about 200 cars a week. At the most, therefore, MGB GT V8 production brought the running total up to only 400 engines a week in total, and Rover had always been able to build more engines than this.

At this point it is worth noting that Rover were preparing for their new SD1 five-door saloon, for which great hopes (and increased sales) were expected, but this car did not go into production until 1976. Between 1973 and 1975, the production of Range Rovers was limited to about 200/250 vehicles a week by the capacity of the single assembly line at Solihull while, as a result of the energy crisis of 1973/4 (and the subsequent steep rise in fuel prices) and the increasing obsolescence of the cars themselves, sales of V8-engined P6Bs fell away steadily.

At no time, therefore, were MG taking more than 10 per cent of Rover V8 engine production, and I doubt very much if they were ever taking more than 6–7 per cent of production capacity. As demand for the Rover saloons fell in 1974 and 1975, it would certainly have been possible for V8 engine production to have swung in favour of the MG, if the demand had been there. In any case, BL had always planned to make the V8 engine also available in the TR7 sports car; the V8 derivative should have been on sale by 1977, but was repeatedly delayed by strikes or by the TR7's failure to sell well enough in North America. There was no increase in V8 engine production capacity in advance of this model's proposed introduction; the big increase came in 1978, when the expansion of Range Rover/Land-Rover facilities at Solihull got under way.

In the late summer of 1973, however, the public knew nothing about this, nor would the vast majority of them have cared, if told. Sales of the MGB GT V8 were encouraging to start with, and (as it later transpired) the model's best monthly production figure of 176 cars was achieved in October 1973. The thousandth example was assembled at Abingdon, just before the end of 1973.

As had been hoped, production of the V8 caused very little disruption at Abingdon. Like the four-cylinder cars, the V8's body shells were pressed and assembled at the Pressed Steel Fisher factory at Swindon, transported to another PSF factory at Cowley (almost passing the MG Abingdon plant on the way) where they were painted and partially trimmed, after which they were transported on huge articulated lorries to Abingdon for final assembly. (As John Thornley has said on more than one occasion, the MG plant at Abingdon was never truly a production facility where things were made, but an assembly facility, where things were screwed together. There was no more obvious case of this way of life than the MGB GT V8, for to join the body shell the engines were trucked in from Rover's Acock's Green factory, while the gearboxes and rear axles were built at the BL transmissions plant at Drews Lane, Birmingham.)

The MGB GT V8, however, was terribly unlucky to be launched in the summer of 1973, for this could not possibly have been arranged at a less propitious moment. For a generation there had been tension, and fighting, in the Middle East. This had erupted into full-scale war in 1956 (which had caused fuel rationing all over Europe), and again in 1967. Now, in 1973, the Arabs and Israelis began yet another conflict, and it had wide-ranging results.

Rightly or wrongly, the Arab nations which controlled almost all Middle East oil production, accused the Western World of favouring the Israeli cause at their expense. Their reaction was not only to place an embargo on oil supplies to some countries, but to double, and then redouble, the well-head price of crude oil pumped out from under their territory. It was the moment at which the OPEC (Organisation of Petroleum Exporting Countries) realised that their control of oil supplies was a formidable political and economic weapon—and this time they resolved to use it. Vain hopes were expressed that the price of oil would be reduced when the conflict was resolved. It never was; indeed, the cost continued to rise, and has done so, inexorably, in the years which followed.

The result, in Britain and in the rest of the Free World, was that the cost and scarcity of fuel increased dramatically, and it also signalled a gradual change in the demand for cars. Almost overnight, it seemed, really large-engined cars began to go out of favour. It did not matter if cars equipped with such large engines were relatively economical; somehow it just seemed to be a bit immoral, or downright unpatriotic, to buy what colloquially became known as a 'gas-guzzler'.

All this, in fact, did not affect the MGB GT V8 as seriously as it might have done, for the car had many features which the British motoring enthusiast recognised, and liked very much. Almost everyone had read the original technical road tests, and had realised that the car's high overall gearing (28.5mph/1,000rpm in overdrive—and don't ever forget that overdrive was standard, while on most of the V8's rivals it was an optional extra) could lead to reasonable fuel economy. *Autocar*, for example, found that at a steady 70mph (the British motorway limit) the MGB GT V8 was consuming 3-star fuel at the miserly rate of only 30.8mpg in overdrive.

Which was all very well towards the end of 1973, when petrol still cost only about 38p a gallon, but things began to look very different during 1974 as prices rocketed alarmingly upwards. By the end of the year petrol cost 75p a gallon, and it was quite clear that more increases were yet to come.

That was bad enough, but the advent of the re-styled Mark II Capri made it even worse. Until then, salesmen in MG dealers' showrooms had at least been able to talk scathingly about the Capri's rather Transatlantic styling, its lack of a hatchback, and its absence of 'breeding'. By 1974, however, not only had Ford established the Capri as a truly formidable racing 'saloon' car (which had won the European Touring Car Championship twice), but they were about to rectify the other deficiencies. From the spring of 1974, MG were in trouble, and within weeks production statistics began to show it. Production ducked under the 100-cars-a-month level temporarily in March 1974, and permanently from June 1974; thereafter the trend was almost entirely downwards.

With the very generous help of MGB GT V8 enthusiasts, Peter Laidler and Geoff Allen, I have been able to assemble the month-by-month production record of the MGB GT V8, which tells its own story. Table 13.2 gives the facts.

Table 13.2 *MGB GT V8—month-by-month production figures, 1972–6*

1972	December	1	Total for Year: 1
1973	January	6	
	February	–	
	March	5	
	April	3	
	May	83	
	June	150	
	July	102	
	August	157	(Public announcement)
	September	105	
	October	176	
	November	146	
	December	98	Total for Year: 1,031
1974	January	142	
	February	145	
	March	75	(Ford Capri Mk II hatchback announced)
	April	124	
	May	122	
	June	94	
	July	29	
	August	58	
	September	18	
	October	20	('Rubber-bumper' model released)
	November	18	
	December	37	Total for Year: 882
1975	January	64	
	February	73	
	March	78	
	April	93	
	May	78	
	June	39	
	July	34	
	August	12	
	September	2	
	October	1	
	November	1	
	December	14	Total for Year: 489
1976	January	42	
	February	43	
	March	39	
	April	39	
	May	15	
	June	6	
	July	2	
	August	1	
	September	1	Total for Year: 188

Note: Each monthly figure is for the number of cars rolling off the *finishing* line at Abingdon. The figures, therefore, differ slightly from the 'official' production statistics published by BL, which were taken at a different point, though the overall totals tally exactly.

The Table shows that, like most new car models, the MGB GT V8 took off with a rush as soon as the public got to know about it. In the 12-month period from June 1973 to May 1974 which, allowing for the inevitable time-lag between building a car and getting it on the road with a customer, just about corresponds to its first full year on the market, a total of 1,542 MGB GT V8s were built, this being more than half, 60 per cent in fact, of all the examples built in the three-year period that the V8-engined car was on sale.

The big drop in production in the autumn of 1974 was not due to a drying-up of sales, but because the MGB GT V8 had to give way to the priority of building four-cylinder MGBs as the complicated change-over to 'black-bumper' styling took place. MGBs built to this style had to be rushed out to North America before the beginning of 1975, and as this was by far MG's most important market, nothing was allowed to interfere with the build-up.

At the same time as the four-cylinder MGB converted from 'chrome bumper' to 'black bumper' style, the MGB GT V8 followed suit, though there was something of an overlap between the types. The last of the 'chrome bumper' MGB GT V8s was Chassis No 1956, completed on 7 October 1974. There was then a considerable gap in the numbering sequence, for the first 'black bumper' car was Chassis No 2101, and no MGB GT V8s were built with intervening numbers. Just to confuse matters, however, the first six 'black bumper' cars—2101 to 2106—were built in August and September before 'chrome bumper' production had ended. This was to allow BL's publicity and service staff to have cars in advance of the start-up of series production; 105 and 106, in fact, were 'show' cars, destined for exhibition at Earls Court in October. True series production of 'black bumper' MGB GT V8s, in fact, did not get under way until the end of October 1974, after a gap of several weeks when no V8-engined cars were being built at all.

From then until September 1976, MGB GT V8 production continued at a diminishing rate, and no further major engineering changes were made to the car. There was, in fact, a further hiccup in the production process, in the autumn of 1975, for the last 1975-model-year car was Chassis No 2632, built on 28 August 1975, while the first 1976-model-year car was Chassis No 2701, not completed until 30 October. There was, therefore, a two-

This is what the 750 'Anniversary Special' four-cylinder MGB GTs looked like when built in 1975. Their specification included the tinted glass and the special road wheels of the MGB GT V8. One V8-engined car, too, was built in this British Racing Green-plus-gold-stripe colour scheme (*BL*)

month period in which no MGB GT V8 cars actually started down the production line, though one or two were still being finished off during that time. The last MGB GT V8 of all was Chassis No 2903, which was finished off on 10 September 1976; it was registered WWL 79R, and is now part of the British Leyland Heritage Collection. This last car, incidentally, was 'non-standard' as far as the normal MGB GT V8 was concerned, in that it was treated to a substantially revised 1977-style facia/instrument/control layout (as found on all 1977–80 four-cylinder MGB models) and the striped seat cover materials. One other car, too, is reputed to have been changed to this style and is now in private hands.

In 1975 (and quite against normal management policy, it seems) one MGB GT V8 (Chassis No 2605) was decked out in the colour scheme of the four-cylinder MGB GT 'Anniversary Special' model, at a time when these special cars, painted British Racing Green, with gold details, were going through the works at Abingdon.

When the decision was taken to drop the V8-engined car, it was not announced with a flourish, for many MG employees were sorry to see these distinctive cars fade away from the scene. But 'fade away' is almost exactly what seemed to happen, for production had been tending gently downwards from the spring of 1976; only fifteen cars were built in May 1976, six in June, two in July, and one car each in August and September. From then on, the fastest, smoothest, most refined, and altogether most delightful MGB of all time was no more.

There has been a constant running battle ever since, verbally and in print, between the followers of the V8s and the followers of the MGCs, about the respective merits of the two cars. MGC fans make the point that their cars might not have been quite as 'sporting' as the four-cylinder MGBs, but that they were mostly very reliable, and provided relaxed high speed cruising. MGB GT V8 enthusiasts, for their part, were full of praise for the sheer urge available from their cars, for their potential fuel economy, for their more predictable handling—although they tended to shy away from the fact that the transmissions had turned out to be rather marginal, and likely to suffer if all the torque of the Rover engine was used all the time. One man—only one, as far as I have been able to ascertain—tried to combine the merits of the two cars, by mating a Rover V8 engine with the structure and suspensions of an MGC, and found that *neither* group of enthusiasts were impressed.

All three types—Twin-Cam, MGC, and MGB GT V8—surely qualify as Mighty MGs. Was the V8-engined the most Mighty of them all?

⑭
Maintaining the MGB GT V8

If ever a car deserved the title of 'Instant Classic', the MGB GT V8 was it. It had every necessary quality—that of being out of the ordinary, of possessing an interesting mechanical layout, of being available in rather limited numbers—and it carried a famous name. It was put on sale in Britain when the cult of the 'classic car' was just being established, and it has continued to be a much talked-about MGB derivative ever since.

It is easy, therefore, to pinpoint the two main reasons why most of the MGB GT V8s ever built are still in existence, and in regular use. One is its 'classic car' status, even while it was being produced, and the other is that it has only recently gone out of production, with the majority of all spare parts still being available.

Of all the 2,591 MGB GT V8s manufactured between 1973 and 1976, it is thought that at least 1,700 cars are still on the road, many in 'like new' condition. However, although nearly all of them were delivered to British customers when they were new, a significant number have subsequently been exported. MGB GT V8s are now to be found in countries like South Africa and Australia, where MG enthusiasm has always been high.

Of the three types of MG surveyed in detail in this book, the MGB GT V8 is always likely to be the one which will be the easiest to repair, restore, or maintain in good condition. This is because the important pressed steel body/chassis unit is very nearly the same as that used in the late-model MGBs (and, from the start-up of 'rubber-bumper' production in the autumn of 1974, many previously unique MGB GT V8 body features were stan-dardised on the four-cylinder car as well), and because the light alloy Rover V8 engine is still in large-scale production, and likely to remain so throughout the 1980s. More than half a million four-cylinder MGBs were built between 1962 and 1980—nearly 200 times as many as the V8-engined derivative—so the supply of common spare parts is assured for many years to come. Broadly speaking, the parts which are already becoming rather difficult to find are the entirely special limited-production items which link one mass-produced item (the engine, say) with another (the body/chassis unit).

In regard to the engine, a few of the unique castings have already gone 'No Longer Available' from BL's Unipart operation, but they are mostly so simple (and made in such cheap metals) that it has been possible to have them re-manufactured. Where it is necessary for this sort of work to be carried out, BL have been prepared to make the necessary drawings available.

The simple way to pick the normal Rover items in the engine from those specially developed for the MG installation is by the quoted part number. Rover parts have all number identifications, special MG-developed components have BHH . . . prefixes and numbers around the 1,000 mark—these are the ones likely to become difficult to find in future years. AHH . . . part numbers are also present, these being earlier MGB four-cylinder car parts in more regular supply and use.

Where the body of the MGB GT V8 uses the same panels as the four-cylinder MGB GT of the 1970s (and this, as already explained in Chapter 12, refers to the vast majority of all items), there should be absolutely no difficulty in obtaining parts. The way to check if any particular panel *is* the same as that used on the four-cylinder cars is to check it out in a BL Parts Manual; the last example I studied covered the four-cylinder and V8 models side by side in the same volume. Incidentally, if the part you need is behind a transverse line through the toeboard/scuttle/windscreen and front door pillars, it is almost certain to be common, and you need check no further.

There is more difficulty in getting reshaped panels around the engine bay, where these were not commonised with 'rubber-bumper' four-cylinder MGBs, but in almost every case the required panel can be produced by modifying a normal MGB item. The oil cooler mounting platform, for instance, which not only had local bulges to clear the extremities of the cooling fan, and mounting holes to locate the cooler itself, can easily be modified from the four-cylinder item by any V8 owner who knows the intimate details of his car.

There may be problems in finding factory-sourced items of soft trim, seat coverings, carpets and the like, simply because the four-cylinder MGB interior was considerably re-styled immediately *after* the MGB GT V8 was phased out of production, and was not significantly changed again in the last four years of the life of the car. MG specialist suppliers in Britain and other countries, however, are already looking after the remanufacture of what I tend to call the 'consumable' items. I need only repeat that, apart from some details of the facia panel itself, all interior trim and furnishing items of the MGB GT V8 were the same as those of the four-cylinder MGB GTs of the period. Nor should there be too much difficulty in finding supplies of the tinted glass—windscreen, doors, quarter windows and back light panels—as this was always an optional extra on late-model MGBs, and was also standardised on the 1975 'Anniversary' MGB GTs, and on the 1980 'Limited Edition' MGB GTs built to commemorate the end of MGB production at Abingdon.

There are some difficulties regarding transmission parts. Complete gearbox/overdrive units are now no longer available, nor are new examples of the gearbox/bell housing casing itself, but all the individual gears, shafts, bearings and related items can be obtained. The Laycock overdrives, of course, are used on several other cars in Britain and Europe and although BL may eventually lose interest in them, Laycock's owners, the Birfield group, provide a very good service back-up.

As I have already made clear, in discussing the other cars surveyed in this book, major component suppliers like Smiths Instruments, Lockheed, and Joseph Lucas (instrument, brake and electrical specialists, respectively) are remarkably helpful to the restorers of older cars like the MGB GT V8, and even when the BL Unipart operation has ceased to stock certain items, it is almost certain that the individual suppliers will still take the trouble to keep owners satisfied.

Apart from the usual troubles which appear with old age on a neglected car (and some MGB GT V8s, surprisingly enough, *have* been neglected)—such as rusting body panels, deteriorating suspension bushes, tatty trim, and missing details—there are only two important areas of design weakness which should be mentioned here. One is relatively minor, the other a much more major consideration.

The minor problem refers to engine mountings. These, on the

V8-engined car, are considerably harder than those fitted to normal MGBs, but they do tend to go soft, allowing the engine to twist more markedly from its normal position. This, in extreme cases, may allow the engine to foul the steering column, setting up vibration problems sounding more serious than, in fact, they are. When buying new mountings, it is far too easy to be fobbed off with normal MGB mounts, so be sure to insist on the right part by quoting the part number.

The problem with the gearbox is that its torque capacity seems to be rather marginal, and that it can only deal with the V8 engine for an indefinite period if it is driven in a sensible manner. Any V8 owner who habitually indulges himself in wheel-spinning starts and crash changes from gear to gear will eventually find that the gears go noisy and that, in extreme cases, teeth may be stripped from the gears altogether. The most vulnerable to trouble is the first motion shaft, that which connects the clutch to the gearbox cluster itself.

There is a simple reason why this should happen, and it all goes back to the very limited budget available to MG and BL engineers when the car was being developed. Although the gear wheels at the rear of the first motion shaft and the front of the layshaft (sometimes known as the constant-mesh or input gears, because they are always engaged and always in use unless direct top gear is selected) were different from those of the four-cylinder MGB, the rest were all exactly the same, and of course exactly the same as those used on the 1968 model-year *non-overdrive* MGCs. The new gears have different numbers of teeth to provide the V8-engined car with approximately 10 per cent closer ratio sets, but the changes go no further than that. From hindsight, therefore, it is quite easy to see why a box stressed originally in the mid-1960s to look after the torque of the 1.8-litre MGB, or the 3.0-litre MGC, should occasionally suffer from the massive torque of the 3.5-litre V8.

Incidentally, although the back axle itself seems to be amply strong enough for its job, even in this car, it seems that supplies of the 3.07:1 crown wheel and pinion gear set are no longer available. MGB GT V8 experts have assured me that, even though this was a Salisbury item, it was not used on any other car except the 1968-model-year MGCs, so it is not to be found by hunting around for parts used in another manufacturer's cars.

At this moment, therefore, what should one keep as spares, on the assumption that parts will eventually become rather more difficult to find, and that certain items tend to be consumables? Peter Laidler, the MGB GT V8 expert who advised me in such detail about these cars, thinks one should have:

A complete set of engine and transmission gaskets
A complete set of water and hydraulic hoses (including those making up the external engine oil circuitry to and from the oil cooler)
Brake pads, linings, and various seals (though Unipart still stock most of these)
Extra spare road wheels (these special Dunlop wheels are no longer made, so take any opportunity you can to aquire extra wheels)
Gearbox internals, particularly the first motion shaft and the lay-gear
A 3.07:1 crown wheel and pinion gear set (*very* rare now)
Soft trim, carpets, and other decorative items

Thus equipped, and with an accurate knowledge of the detailed engineering of his car, the MGB GT V8 owner can look forward to many years of shortage-free motoring.

Incidentally, because the location and number of specialists seem to change very rapidly these days, I do not propose to provide a list, which would be correct only for the summer of 1981, when this book is being written. I should, however, say that there are two important contacts for V8 owners—the MG Owners Club, whose headquarters are in Swavesey, near Cambridge, and the Beer of Houghton organisation, who have probably as much MG expertise as any other organisation, and an impressive stock of V8 parts.

APPENDIX A

Twin-Cam, MGC and MGB GT V8 Colours

There is no new information in this short Appendix, which merely groups together the colour/trim combinations available on the Mighty MGs. Most enthusiasts like to keep their 'classic' cars in 'original' condition, and of course for the Concours competitor it is absolutely essential that this should be so. Details are as follows:

Body Paint Colour	Hood	Interior Trim

Twin-Cam Tourer (to Ch No 2192)

Body Paint Colour	Hood	Interior Trim
Ash Green		Grey or Black
Black		Red or Green
Glacier Blue	Black or Ice Blue	Grey or Black
Old English White		Red or Black
Orient Red		Red or Black

(from Ch No 2193)

Ash Green, Glacier Blue and Orient Red were dropped, and replaced by:

Alamo Beige	Beige	Red
Chariot Red	Beige or Grey	Beige, Red or Black
Dove Grey	Grey	Red
Iris Blue	Blue	Black

Twin-Cam Coupe (to Ch No 2291)

Ash Green	—	Grey or Black
Black	—	Red or Green
Glacier Blue	—	Grey or Black
Old English White	—	Red or Black
Orient Red	—	Red or Black

(from Ch No 2292)

Ash Green, Glacier Blue and Orient Red were dropped, and replaced by:

Alamo Beige	—	Red
Chariot Red	—	Red or Black
Dove Grey	—	Red
Iris Blue	—	Black

It was also, of course, possible to specify certain special colours such as British Racing Green if an extra price was paid.

The change-over in colour choice occurred at Abingdon when the MGA 1500 model was dropped, and replaced by the revised MGA 1600 model. Twin-Cams were given the new colour combinations and the new styling details of the 1600s at the same time.

199

MGC (Eight colours for both body types, Golden Beige, Grampian Grey and Sandy Beige for Coupes only).

Body Paint Colour	Hood	Interior Trim
Black	Black or Grey	Black
British Racing Green	Black or Grey	Black
Golden Beige	—	Black
Grampian Grey	—	Black or Red
Mineral Blue	Black	Black or Blue
Old English White	Black	Black or Red
Pale Primrose	Black	Black
Riviera Blue	Black	Black
Sandy Beige	—	Black or Red
Snowberry White	Black	Black
Tartan Red	Black	Black

Other special colours were available on occasional cars. Note that most University Motors Specials had their own distinctive colour schemes.

MGB GT V8

All cars, of course, were GTs, so there is no 'Hood' column.

Body Paint Colour	Interior Trim
Aconite	Autumn Leaf
Black	Autumn Leaf or Black
Black Tulip	Autumn Leaf or Ochre
Blaze	Navy or Black
Bracken	Autumn Leaf
Bronze Yellow	Navy
Brooklands Green	Autumn Leaf
Chartreuse	Black
Citron	Black
Damask Red	Navy or Black
Flamenco Red	Black
Glacier White	Autumn Leaf, Navy or Black
Green Mallard	Autumn Leaf or Ochre
Harvest Gold	Navy or Black
Lime Flower	Navy
Mirage	Black
Police White	Navy or Black
Sandglow	Autumn Leaf
Tahiti Blue	Autumn Leaf
Teal Blue	Autumn Leaf or Ochre
Tundra	Autumn Leaf

There was a single 'Anniversary Special' in 1975:

British Racing Green (with Gold Flash)	Black

APPENDIX B

Technical Specifications

MGA Twin-Cam—built 1958 to 1960

Engine
Configuration:
Four cylinders, in line, mounted vertically in car.

Bore, stroke and capacity:
75.39 × 88.9mm, 1,588cc (2.97 × 3.50in, 96.9cu in)

Compression ratio:
9.9:1 at first, 8.3:1 from Chassis No 2251 (Autumn 1959). Many earlier engines subsequently converted to 8.3:1.

Maximum power:
108bhp (nett) at 6,700rpm on 9.9:1 compression ratio. 100bhp (nett) at 6,700rpm on 8.3:1 compression ratio.

Maximum torque:
104lb ft at 4,500rpm on 9.9:1 compression ratio. Figures for lowered-compression engine never revealed.

Induction system:
Two constant vacuum SU carburettors, mounted semi-downdraught at 22.5 degrees from horizontal, with 1.75in chokes, type H6. Wire-mesh Vokes air filters. SU high-pressure fuel pump. 10 Imperial gallon (45.5 litre) fuel tank; no reserve.

Valve gear:
Twin overhead camshafts; two-stage drive by primary helical gears, and by secondary duplex chain, with manual and automatic adjustment. Shim-adjusted inverted bucket-type tappets, and double coil springs. Two valves per cylinder—one inlet, one exhaust—symmetrically disposed at 80 degree included angle.

Lubrication:
Wet sump, capacity 12 Imperial pints (5.7 litres). Gear-driven Hobourn Eaton oil pump, full-flow oil filter, and optional oil cooler.

Ignition:
Lucas coil and distributor, with contact breaker. 14mm sparking plugs, one per cylinder.

Materials:
Cast-iron cylinder block/crankcase, no cylinder liners. Three-bearing forged steel crankshaft, with torsional vibration damper at crank nose. Main and big-end bearings steel shells with lead-indium flashing. Forged steel connecting rods. Cast light-alloy pistons with circlip located gudgeon pins. Light-alloy sump casting, camshaft covers, and inlet manifolds. Cast-iron exhaust manifold. Cast light-alloy cylinder head with austenitic iron valve seats; part spherical shaped combustion chambers.

Transmission
Gearbox:
Four-speed BMC B-Series manual gearbox, with cast-iron casing. Synchromesh on top, third and second gears. Central, remote-control gear change. 8.0in single-dry-plate Borg and Beck clutch.

No overdrive option, nor automatic transmission option.

Internal gearbox ratios: 1.00, 1.374, 2.214, 3.64, reverse 4.76:1. Optional close-ratio gears available for competition use.

Rear axle/final drive:
BMC B-Series rear axle, 'banjo' type construction. Hypoid bevel final drive and differential, of BMC manufacture. Final drive ratio 4.3:1. Optional ratios, higher or lower, available for competition use.

Gearing:
17.3mph/1,000 in top gear. Theoretical top speed at peak power, 115.9mph.

Chassis
Type:
Separate pressed-steel chassis frame, with box section side members and scuttle bracing, with pressed, box and tubular cross-bracings.

Front suspension:
Independent by upper and lower wishbones, with coil springs. No anti-roll bar in standard form at first, standard from Ch No 2275. Armstrong hydraulic lever arm dampers, with arm doubling as linkage for 'upper wishbone'.

Rear suspension:
Live axle, half-elliptic leaf springs, and Armstrong hydraulic lever arm dampers. No further axle location.

Steering:
Cam gear rack-and-pinion, with 16.5in four-spoke 'sprung' steering wheel.

Wheels and tyres:
Dunlop pressed-steel disc wheels, with 4.0in (114mm) rim width, and centre-lock attachment to hubs by 'knock-on' ears. 5.90–15in Dunlop RS4 cross-ply tyres.

Brakes:
Dunlop disc brakes at front *and* rear, hydraulically operated, with separate mechanically operated caliper for hand brake to rear discs. Two pads per brake, with quick change facility. Single hydraulic circuit, no servo assistance. Disc diameters 10.75in (273mm) front and rear. Swept areas 247.4sq in (1,596sq cm) at front and rear. 'Fly off' type handbrake.

Body
Type:
Two-seater style, available in open tourer or closed 'bubble-top' Coupe versions. Two passenger doors, separate boot lid and luggage accommodation.

Details:
Both bodies built from pressed-steel panels, except for pressed light-alloy bonnet, boot lid, and door skin panels. By Morris Bodies Branch, Coventry.
Open tourer version with fixed windscreen, removable perspex side screens, and separate hood sticks and fabric hood.
Coupe version with wrap-around windscreen style, permanently fixed pressed-steel hardtop, wrap-around rear window, and glass wind-up side windows.
For the Tourer version, an optional detachable hardtop was available, originally in light-alloy, later in glass fibre.
Heater installation optional.
Seats could be folded forward if required, but did not recline.

Optional equipment:
Included heater/demister for cold climates, cold air ventilation for hot climates, radio, adjustable length steering column, tonneau cover (for Tourer), competition windscreen (low—for Tourer), hardtop (for Tourer), oil cooler, sliding sidescreens (for Tourer), various 'Competition' equipment and other 'comfort' options.

Dimensions:
Wheelbase 7ft 10in (2,388mm)
Front track 3ft 11.9in (1,216mm)

Rear track 4ft 0.9in (1,242mm)
Overall length 13ft 0in (3,962mm)
Overall width 4ft 9.25in (1,454mm)
Overall height (unladen) 4ft 2in (1,270mm)
Unladen weight (Tourer) 2,185lb (991kg)
Unladen weight (Coupe) 2,245lb (1,018kg)

British Price (Basic)
Tourer £843
Coupe £904

MGC—built 1967 to 1969

Engine
Configuration:
Six cylinders, in line, mounted vertically in car.

Bore, stroke and capacity:
83.36 × 88.9mm, 2,912cc (3.28 × 3.50in, 177.7cu in)

Compression ratio:
9.0:1

Maximum power:
145bhp (nett) at 5,250rpm

Maximum torque:
170lb ft at 3,400rpm

Induction system:
Two constant vacuum SU carburettors, mounted horizontally, with 1.75in chokes, type HS6. Paper element air cleaners. SU electric fuel pump. 12 Imperial gallon (54.8 litres) fuel tank; no reserve.
Valve gear:
Single camshaft, mounted in side of cylinder block, driven from nose of crankshaft by duplex chain, with automatic adjustment. Line of valves, overhead mounted in cylinder head, operated by pushrods

and rockers from side-mounted camshaft. Double valve springs. Two valves per cylinder—one inlet, one exhaust.

Lubrication:
Wet sump, capacity 12.8 Imperial pints (7.2 litres). Gear-driven Concentric oil pump, full-flow oil filter, and oil cooler mounted ahead of water radiator.

Ignition:
Lucas coil and distributor, with contact breaker. 14mm sparking plugs, one per cylinder.

Materials:
Cast-iron cylinder block/crankcase, no cylinder liners. Seven-bearing forged-steel crankshaft, with torsional vibration damper at nose. Main and big-end bearings, steel shells flashed with reticular tin. Forged-steel connecting rods. Cast light-alloy pistons with circlip fitted gudgeon pins. Pressed-steel sump pan, and valve gear cover. Cast alloy front engine cover. Cast light-alloy inlet manifolds. Cast-iron exhaust manifolds. Cast-iron

203

cylinder head, with cast-in provision for exhaust air injection (to suit USA exhaust-emission requirements). BMC-Weslake kidney-shaped combustion chambers.

Transmission
Four-speed all-synchromesh manual gearbox standard, with optional Laycock overdrive, or optional Borg Warner Type 35 three-speed automatic transmission.

Manual gearbox:
Four-speed BMC manual gearbox, with cast alloy casing. Synchromesh on all forward gears. Gearbox selectors mounted in side of casing, but central, remote-control gear change. 9.0in diameter diaphragm spring Borg and Beck clutch.
Internal gearbox ratios:
Original manual, *non*-overdrive cars 1.00, 1.382, 2.167, 3.44, reverse 3.095:1. Original cars fitted with overdrive, and all manual transmission cars built from Ch No 4236 (GT) and 4266 (Tourer) 1.00, 1.307, 2.058, 2.98, reverse 2.679:1. Optional close ratios for competition use.

Optional overdrive:
Laycock Type LH, operating on top and third gears, with facia-mounted switch. (Column-mounted on US-market cars) 0.82:1 ratio.

Automatic transmission:
Borg Warner Type 35, with torque converter, three forward ratios, and reverse. Central, remote control, range change lever. Internal gear ratios 1.00–2.20, 1.45–3.19, 2.39–5.26, reverse 2.09–4.60:1.

Maximum torque multiplication 2.20:1.

Rear axle/final drive:
BMC Salisbury-type axle, with central cast-iron casing, and steel side tubes. Hypoid bevel final drive and differential, by Salisbury.

Final drive ratios:
Original cars:
Non-overdrive 3.07:1, overdrive and automatic gearbox 3.31:1.
From Chassis No 4236 (GT), and 4266 (Tourer): Non-overdrive and automatic gearbox 3.31:1, overdrive gearbox 3.7:1.
Other ratios, mainly numerically higher, available for competition use, along with optional limited slip differential.

Gearing:
With 3.07:1 differential, 23.85mph/1,000rpm in direct top gear.
With 3.31:1 differential, 22.1mph/1,000rpm in direct top gear, 27.0mph/1,000rpm in overdrive top.
With 3.7:1 differential, 19.8mph/1,000rpm in direct top gear, 24.1mph/1,000rpm in overdrive top.

Chassis
Type:
Unit-construction pressed-steel body-chassis shell, in open tourer or fastback GT form.

Front suspension:
Independent by upper and lower wishbones, with longitudinal torsion bars, adjustable for height setting. Anti-roll bar. Telescopic hydraulic dampers.

Rear suspension:
Live axle, half-elliptic leaf springs,

and hydraulic lever-arm dampers. No further axle location.

Steering:
Cam gear rack and pinion, with 16.5in three-spoke 'sprung' steering wheel. Energy-absorbing steering column for North American market, fixed-length column for other markets.

Wheels and tyres:
Choice of types. Basic specification, pressed steel disc wheels, with five-stud fixing. Optional, Dunlop centre-lock wire-spoke wheels, with attachment by 'knock-on' ears or nuts (non-UK markets), or (from 4236 [GT] and 4266 [Tourer]) optional Rostyle disc wheels, with five-stud fixing. All with 5.0in (127mm) rim width. 165-15in radial ply Dunlop SP41 tyres at first; from 4236 (GT) and 4266 (Tourer) 165HR15 radial-ply Dunlop SP68 tyres.

Brakes:
Girling system, front wheel disc brakes, and rear wheel drums, hydraulically operated, with separate cable-operated handbrake. Two pads per disc brake, with quick change facility. Leading and trailing shoes to rear drum brakes.
Single hydraulic circuit most markets, split hydraulic circuit for North American markets, with vacuum servo assistance. Two servos for North American market. Disc diameter 11.06in (281mm), rear drum diameter 9.0in, with 2.5in wide brake shoes (229 × 63.5mm).
Swept areas, front 226.2sq in, rear 127.2sq in (1,459sq cm and 821sq cm).

Body
Type:
Two types—available as two-seater open tourer, or as 2+2 seater closed GT model. Two passenger doors on all versions, with large glass hatchback on GT derivative. Separate luggage accommodation and boot lid for Tourer, luggage space in same compartment along with passenger accommodation in GT version.

Details:
Both bodies, in unit with chassis, built from pressed steel panels, welded together, but with pressed light-alloy bonnet skin panels (few cars built with steel skin panels). Assembly of shell by Pressed Steel Co, Swindon.
Open-tourer version with fixed windscreen, and separate hood sticks, and fabric hood. GT version with fixed steel fastback hardtop, sweeping down to the tail, incorporating large hinged lift-up glass hatchback.
Both cars with wind-up glass side windows and swivelling front quarter windows.
Optional heater installation.
Seats folded forward. From 4236 (GT) and 4266 (Tourer) provision for reclining was included; previous to this the seat angle was fixed. In GT version, backrest of occasional '+2' seat could be folded forward to extend the rear loading platform.
For Tourer version, glass-fibre detachable hardtop was optionally available.

Optional equipment:
Included heater/demister, cold-air equipment (Australia only), hardtop, tonneau cover, folding 'Pack-

away' hood (Tourer), heated rear screen (GT), various 'Competition' equipment and other 'comfort' options.

Dimensions:
Wheelbase 7ft 7in (2,311mm)
Front track 4ft 2in (1,270mm)
Rear track 4ft 1.25in (1,251mm)
Overall length 12ft 9.2in (3,891mm)
Overall width 5ft 0in (1,524mm)
Overall height (unladen) Tourer 4ft 2.25in (1,276mm)

Overall height (unladen) GT 4ft 3in (1,295mm)
Unladen weight (Tourer) 2,460lb (1,116kg)
Unladen weight (GT) 2,610lb (1,184kg)

British Price (Basic)
Tourer, £895 at first, £924 from May 1968, £937 from January 1969
GT, £1,015 at first, £1,045 from May 1968, £1,057 from January 1969

MGB GT V8—Built 1973 to 1976

Engine
Configuration:
Eight cylinders, in 90 degree vee formation, symmetrically mounted in car.

Bore, stroke and capacity:
88.9 × 71.1mm, 3,528cc (3.50 × 2.80in, 215.4cu in)

Compression ratio:
8.25:1

Maximum power:
137bhp (DIN) at 5,000rpm

Maximum torque:
193lb ft at 2,900rpm

Induction system:
Two constant vacuum SU carburettors, horizontally mounted, with 1.75in chokes, type HIF6. Two paper element air cleaners. SU high-pressure fuel pump. 12 Imperial gallons (54 litres) fuel tank; no reserve.

Valve gear:
Single camshaft, mounted in 'vee' of cylinder block, driven by inverted tooth chain from nose of crankshaft. Automatically adjusted

hydraulic tappets. Line of valves in each cylinder head, overhead mounted, operated by pushrods and rockers from centrally mounted camshaft. Double valve springs. Two valves per cylinder—one inlet, one exhaust.

Lubrication:
Wet sump, capacity 8 Imperial pints (4.5 litres). Gear-driven Hobourn Eaton oil pump, full-flow oil filter, with oil cooler mounted ahead of water radiator.

Ignition:
Lucas coil and distributor, with contact breaker. 14mm sparking plugs, one per cylinder.

Materials:
Cast light-alloy cylinder block/crankcase, with press-fit centrifugally cast steel cylinder liners. Five-bearing spheroidal cast-iron crankshaft, with torsional vibration damper at nose. Main and big-end bearings, steel shells, with lead-indium flashing. Forged steel connecting rods. Cast light-alloy pistons with interference-fit gudgeon pin fixings. Pressed-steel oil

sump pan. Cast light-alloy rocker covers and front cover. Cast light-alloy inlet manifold and inlet plenum chamber. Cast-iron exhaust manifolds. Cast light-alloy cylinder heads, with cast-iron valve seats, incorporating part-spherical combustion chambers.

Transmission
Four-speed all-synchromesh manual gearbox with Laycock overdrive. No options.

Gearbox:
Four-speed BMC manual gearbox, with cast-alloy casing. Synchromesh on all forward gears. Gear selectors in side of gearbox, but central, remote control gear change.
9.5in diameter diaphragm spring Borg and Beck clutch.
Internal gearbox ratios 1.00, 1.259, 1.974, 3.138, reverse 2.819:1.

Overdrive:
Laycock Type LH unit, operating only on top gear. 0.82:1 ratio, with operation by steering-column-mounted switch.

Rear axle/final drive:
BMC Salisbury axle, with cast-iron central casing, and steel side tubes. Hypoid bevel final drive and differential, by Salisbury. Final drive ratio 3.07:1. Other ratios available for competition use, along with limited slip differential.

Gearing:
23.4mph/1,000rpm in direct top gear.
28.5mph/1,000rpm in overdrive top gear.

Chassis
Type:
Unit-construction, pressed-steel body/chassis shell, only available in fastback GT form, built by Pressed Steel Fisher at Swindon.

Front suspension:
Independent by upper and lower wishbones, with coil springs and anti-roll bar. Armstrong hydraulic lever-arm dampers, with arm doubling as linkage for upper 'wishbone'.

Rear suspension:
Live axle, half-elliptic leaf springs, and Armstrong hydraulic lever-arm dampers. No further axle location.

Steering:
Cam gear rack-and-pinion, with collapsible steering column to meet safety legislation, and 15.5in diameter alloy-spoked simulated leather-rimmed steering wheel.

Wheels and tyres:
Sculptured Dunlop wheels, with four-stud fixing, having ventilated cast-alloy centres riveted to steel rims. 5.0in rim width. 175HR14in radial ply tyres, of various makes.

Brakes:
Lockheed brakes, front wheel discs and rear wheel drums, hydraulically operated, with separate cable-operated handbrake. Two pads per disc brake, with quick change facility. Leading and trailing shoes to rear drum brakes. Single hydraulic circuit (split circuit on the seven left-hand-drive cars), with vacuum servo assistance. Disc diameter 10.7in (272mm), rear drum diameter 10.0in with 1.7in wide shoes (254 × 43mm). Swept areas, front 231.6sq in, rear 106.8sq in (1,494 sq cm and 689sq cm)

Body

Type:
One type—2+2 seater closed GT model, with two passenger doors, and large glass hatchback. No separate luggage compartment. No open tourer version.

Details:
Body shell in unit with chassis, built from pressed-steel panels, welded together, with pressed-steel bonnet skin panel. Fixed windscreen, and fixed steel fast-back hardtop, sweeping down to the tail, incorporating a large hinged lift-up hatchback, mainly glass. Wind-up glass side windows. Heater installation standard. Seats folded forward if required, and could also partially be reclined.

The backrest of the occasional '+2' seat could be folded forward to extend the rear loading platform.

Optional equipment:
Radio installation.

Dimensions:
Wheelbase 7ft 7.1in (2,315mm)
Front track 4ft 1in (1,244mm)
Rear track 4ft 1.25in (1,251mm)
Overall length (to Chassis No 1956) 12ft 10.7in (3,929mm)
Overall length (from Chassis No 2101) 13ft 2.25in (4,020mm)
Overall width 5ft 0in (1,524mm)
Overall height 4ft 2in (1,270mm)
Unladen weight 2,442lb (1,108kg)

British Price (Basic)
£1,925 on announcement in 1973, rising rapidly to £3,317 when discontinued in 1976.

APPENDIX C

Identifying the Breed

Accurate identification of a particular car is always valuable. It gives an existing owner a good idea of the period in which his car was built, and it lets a potential customer know that he is looking at 'the real thing' when he goes out shopping.

Agreed, it would be virtually impossible for a sharp operator to construct an MGC out of the remains of an MGB, but it would not be very difficult for a Twin-Cam to be 'cloned', nor even for an MGB GT V8 to evolve from the the basis of a four-cylinder MGB of the period.

Table C.1, therefore, and the notes which accompany it, should accurately define any of the three model ranges considered in this book.

In preparing this table, I have tried to be super-accurate, not to say pedantic, and have consulted the MG chassis-build records for the purpose, which are now lodged with BL Heritage. In the case of the MGA Twin-Cam there is no possible confusion, but the story is a little less clear-cut as far as the start-up of production of MGCs and MGB GT V8s are concerned.

The MGC chassis books list cars from No 101, but it is also made clear that the first fourteen cars (..101 to ..114) were all 'Allocated to Development Department'; most of those first cars were built at the end of 1966, or in the early months of 1967. *True* quantity production was delayed until October/November 1967, with the first few cars being allocated to the Press Demonstration fleet.

The tiny overlap between 1968 and 1969 model-year cars was unavoidable in view of the fact that open cars and GTs were being built down the same production line. The total overlap, in any case, is no more than 30 cars, which represents rather more than a single day's production.

As with the MGC, so with the MGB GT V8. The first car listed in the Chassis book was finshed before the end of 1972, in fact on 12 December 1972, and a further 12 pre-production cars were all started before the end of January 1973. True quantity production began with Chassis Number . .114, which was completed on 27 March 1973.

In the case of the MGB GT V8, there are two gaps in the Chassis Number sequence. The last 'chrome bumper' car was . .1956, and the first 'black-bumper' car was . .2101. The last 1975-model-year car was . .2632, and the first 1976-model-year car was . .2701. It follows that if anyone offers you a GT V8 with chassis number between 1957 and 2100, or 2633 and 2700, it is a fake! There was no good reason for this, except that it was administratively rather tidy to tackle a significant technical junction this way.

Incidentally, in some cases there may have been a lengthy interval between the actual completion of a car and its delivery to a customer, so I must emphasise that the months quoted above are for the point at which the car in question was driven off the Finishing Line at Abingdon. In the case of the MGC, for instance, it is known that the last car was built in September 1969, but it is also known that the last car did not *leave* Abingdon until March 1970, more than five months later.

In addition to the range of chassis numbers, the following should positively identify each type of car.

MGA Twin-Cam

Original destination when new: The identifying chassis number prefixes, YD, or YM, were always followed by /1, /2, /3 or /5, and these in turn were followed by the number itself.

A car marked: /1 was right-hand-drive, for Home market delivery
     /2 was right-hand-drive, for Export delivery
     /3 was left-hand-drive, for Export delivery
     /5 was a CKD car

The Chassis Number itself was stamped on a plate which was mounted on the bulkhead shelf behind the engine.

The Engine Number was stamped on a metal plate fixed to the rear of the cylinder block, above the bell housing machined face.

An example of the number would be: 16GB/U/2127, where 16 referred to the 1.6-litre size, G to its use in an MG, B to the fact that it was a B-Series derived engine, and U to the fact that a centre gearchange was fitted.

The Gearbox Number was stamped on top of the gearbox casing, to the left of the gearbox dipstick, and near the filler plug. A typical number

Table C.1 *Chassis Numbers*

Model	First Chassis Number	Important Interim Chassis Number	Final Chassis Number	When Built	Notes
MGA Twin-Cam	YD YM } ...501			June 1958	D = Tourer, M = Coupe
		..2251		June 1959	First car with reduced compression ratio (8.3:1) engine
			..2611	June 1960	
MGC	GCN ..101 GCD ..110 }			November 1966	N = Tourer, D = GT
		..114		July 1967	Pre-production car
		D..4236 N..4266		October/ November 1968	First true quantity-production car
			N..9099 D..9102	September 1969	First revised 1969 models, with different gearing, seat recline, etc
MGB GT V8	GD2D...101	GD2D...114		December 1972	Pre-production car
		GD2D..1956		March 1973	First true quantity-production car
		GD2D..2101		October 1974	Last 'chrome-bumper' car
		GD2D..2632		August 1974	First 'black-bumper' car
		GD2D..2701		August 1975	Last 1975 model year car
				October 1975	First 1976 model-year car
			GD2D..2903	September 1976	

would be A2336, and it would be impossible to see from underneath the car with the gearbox correctly installed. The box, incidentally, is the same in all internal respects as that fitted to the pushrod-engined model.

The Back Axle Number was stamped on the front of the axle case, near the left-hand spring seat.

The Body Number which was by no means the same as the Chassis Number, nor by any means as significant, was stamped on a metal plate fixed to the bulkhead in the engine bay, close to the right-hand bonnet hinge.

MGC

Chassis Numbers were on a plate fixed to the left-hand valance in the engine bay, facing the engine. A typical number would be prefixed by GCN1L.... or GCD1U...., where G meant that the car was an MG, C meant that a C-Series engine was in use, N or D meant that a Tourer or GT body shell was fitted, 1 meant the First Series (there never was a second series), and L or U (where marked) meant that the car had left-hand-drive, or was destined for the United States.

Engine Numbers were fixed to the cylinder block, just below the cylinder head machined face, close to the rear of the alternator. A typical number would be 29G/U/H (or, in the cars for the United States, 29GA/U/H.....), where the 29 denotes 2.9-litres, G means the MG application, U denotes a centre gearchange, and H denotes a high-compression engine.

Gearbox Numbers give no identification of the different sets of ratios employed on this model. The number itself is of no relevance, and is stamped on the casing, on the near-side, under the cover for the selector mechanism at the side of the box.

Back Axle Numbers, like those of the Twin-Cam, are stamped on the left-side casing, but there is no identification of which of the three ratios is installed.

Body Numbers are on a plate secured to the left-hand inner valance, facing the carburettors and air cleaners.

University Motors Specials—and Downton conversions
Mosts UMs differed in detail from each other, but the following points should be noted:

A genuine Downton conversion has a special identifying engine number stamped on the cylinder head. If the Stage 3 triple-SU installation is present it is identified by the mounting of the carburettors at a downdraught angle, rather than being upright.

(Some Downton conversions were applied to earlier cars, but the genuine UM connection was not established until the summer of 1969.)

All UMs had special paint-jobs (some two-tone), special badges to bonnet or front wings, Motolita steering wheels, chrome rocker covers and chrome oil-filter covers.

Many had the front bonnet bulge painted matt black, many had special road wheels (some even had light-alloy knock-ons), and many had Koni shock absorbers.

Some cars had Downton engine conversions, several had MGB Mk II vinyl seats, but only a few had the special slatted front grille.

MGB GT V8

Chassis Numbers were to be found on a plate riveted to the inner engine bay valance very close to the engine oil filter, on the right-hand side of the engine. A typical number was prefixed by: GD2D1 or GD2D2..., where G meant that this was an MG, D meant that an engine of more than 3,000cc was installed, 2 meant that the body had two-passenger doors, the second D meant that it was a GT body shell, and 1 or 2 referred to the use of right-hand-drive or left-hand-drive respectively.

Engine Numbers were stamped on the left side of the cylinder block, near the rear machined face. Typically they were prefixed 486...., which was a Rover number used for this engine type.

Gearbox Numbers were stamped on the top of the casing, quite invisible from underneath the car, and were prefixed by the letter A.

Back Axle Numbers, as with the other models covered in this book, were stamped on the left-side tube.

Body Numbers were to be found on the bonnet landing platform, ahead of the water radiator.

APPENDIX D

Production and Deliveries—Year by Year Analysis

To a romantic, the breakdown of Mighty MG production, by year and by market, may be a boring irrelevance. To a historian, however, it may be extremely revealing. To the present-day enthusiast, of course, the chronicle of where the cars were delivered when new might also be a guide to where most of the surviving examples are to be found.

To assemble the tables in this Appendix, I have been able to examine the MG archive material now held by BL Heritage, and I am very grateful for their help in this analysis. What is rather infuriating, however, is that in the case of the MGC statistics there is a slight but irritating discrepancy between the annual production breakdown and the number and type of each car built. To be specific, somewhere along the line the hard-working analysts at Abingdon managed to 'lose' a total of 23 cars, and I cannot satisfactorily explain this. It seems certain that 8,999 MGCs were built, but the market-by-market analysis provided mentions only 8,976—the short-fall being 15 Tourers and 8 GTs.

Table D.1, therefore, is that of Total Deliveries, broken down into Home, Export, CKD kit, and United States sections.

More than anything else, this table emphasises the importance of the United States market to the MG marque, and it spotlights the commer-

Table D.1 *Total deliveries*

	Home	Export RHD	Export LHD	CKD RHD	CKD LHD	Export USA	Total
MGA Twin-Cam	360	199	384	96	37	1,035	2,111
MGC (1968 model)	2,331	93	494	—	—	1,207	4,125
MGC (1969 model)*	1,099	65	652	—	—	3,035	4,851
MGB GT V8	2,584	—	—	—	—	7**	2,591

Note: CKD = Completely Knocked Down kits.

* 1969 model MGCs began at Ch No 4236 (GT) and 4266 (Tourer).

** As explained in the text, these seven cars were among the first ten MGB GT V8 production cars, and were built entirely to USA-specification. None was sold in the USA, but eventually went to owners in Europe.

cial lunacy of British Leyland in confining the MGB GT V8 to the British market alone. In three years, fewer V8s were sold in Britain than the MGC achieved in less than two years, and without export sales there could never have been any prospect for the model.

The table also shows that without the benefit of the United States market the export success of these MGs would have been very limited indeed.

Clearly the MGA Twin-Cam is much the rarest domestic-market Mighty MG; and that rarity has almost certainly increased in recent years as some of the surviving cars have been sold to North America.

Table D.2, which spotlights demand for the various body styles, is equally illuminating.

Table D.2 *Production of body type*

	Open Tourer	Closed Coupe/GT
MGA Twin-Cam	1,801	310
MGC (1968 model)	2,125	2,000
MGC (1969 model)	2,402	2,449
MGB GT V8	—	2,591

Throughout the 1950s and 1960s, all over the world there was a steady fall in the demand for open-air motoring, nowhere more obvious than in the sports-car market. It was not only in Britain, but also in Europe and North America, that sales departments found their customers beginning to prefer to motor in warmth, relative silence, and protected from the weather, rather than braving the elements and the increasingly fouls-melling air on congested roads.

The fact that the MGB GT V8 was never made available with an open-tourer body style does not help to make a conclusive analysis of MG trends possible. However, I have never completely been convinced that an open V8 was never marketed because of structural limitations, in spite of what V8 enthusiasts have suggested. On the other hand, I am sure that the GT-only policy was followed because of unmistakable market trends, and because of the threat of impending legislation against open cars, not least in North America. (The fact that, in the end, the V8 was never marketed in North America—where it would have competed head-on with the BL Triumph Stag—made a nonsense of this!)

I should point out, however, that although only 15 per cent of MGA Twin-Cams were closed Coupes, about half of all MGC production was of GTs. In view of the experience of large concerns like Datsun (with the 240Z), Alfa Romeo (with the Giulias) and Fiat (with the 124 Sports), it seems certain that the majority of MGB GT V8 sales *would* have been for closed cars, even if an open version had been on offer.

Year-by-year production figures are also illuminating, and in this case I should emphasise that the 'official' MGC production total of 8,999 is confirmed.

Table D.3 *Annual Production*

	MGA Twin-Cam	MGC Tourer	MGC GT	MGB GT V8
1958	541			
1959	1,519			
1960	51			
1967		189	41	
1968		2,566	2,462	
1969		1,787	1,954	
1972				3*
1973				1,069
1974				854
1975				489
1976				176

* First three pre-production cars. True quantity production began in March 1973.

What is truly significant here is that production (and, by inference, sales) of Twin-Cams had died away almost completely by the end of 1959, and that V8 production (and sales) tended steadily downwards after the first-year demand had been satisfied. The MGC, however, was selling steadily (if not spectacularly) throughout its short life. *Average* MGC production in 1968 was at the rate of 420 cars a month; cars were only in production for the first eight months of 1969, so the average figure for that year was nearly 470. I cannot believe, I truly cannot, that the MGC was withdrawn because it was not selling well enough. *All* the evidence was that it was a good car to have in the range. Dare I suggest that it was withdrawn because it was something of a nuisance to build at Abingdon, and that it might be considered as a competitor to the Triumph Stag, which was about to be launched in 1970?

Incidentally, the old *canard* which states that the V8 was always hampered by a lack of engine supplies from Rover in Solihull does not really stand up to close scrutiny. For one thing, Rover continued supplying Morgan with engines for their Plus 8 sports car (and, in 1976, let's not forget, *more* Plus 8s were being built than MGB GT V8s!), and for another the number of V8-engined Rovers being built steadily *fell* from 1973 to 1976, which meant that the engine-building capacity at Rover was by no means stretched. MGB GT V8 enthusiasts will probably not agree with me, but my conclusion is that the British customer really did not want to buy the V8—or, at least, he did not want to buy a second one, having bought the first. I must also repeat the point made in the text, that from March 1974 the MGB GT V8 had a formidable competitor in the Capri 3-litre Mk II, which not only had similar performance, but had four almost full-size seats, and was considerably cheaper.

215

APPENDIX E

Performance Data—All Types

How many enthusiasts buy a famous type of older car, fall in love with it, and begin to believe the exaggerated claims often made for its performance? Too many, I'm afraid. It is for that reason, above all, that I like to publish a summary of the performance figures recorded for the cars when they were in quantity production, *by unbiased* sources.

Because the three distinct types of 'Mighty MGs' were mechanically so different from each other, a cross comparison is very interesting and informative. Might I even suggest that the long-running arguments between the MGC and MGB GT V8 fans should now be ended, and that the true worth of the MGA Twin-Cam can now be assessed?

Although only three models are involved, there was no lack of variety in the cars tested. I have felt it right to extract figures from Britain's *only* two authoritative motoring magazines—*Autocar* and *Motor*—in the case of the standard production cars. In each case, their staff go to considerable lengths to carry out an impartial test; they never take a manufacturer's claims on trust, and they never fudge the figures to produce a preconceived impression. It is therefore quite right and proper that there should be differences in the statistics presented, for the simple reason that the cars used were different, were tested on different days in different weather conditions, and were driven by different testers.

In each case, directly comparable figures are available for cars with manual transmission, although in the case of the MGC it was only *Autocar* which was given a chance to 'figure' the automatic transmission version. In addition to these cars, I have also extracted performance figures for the 'Costello' V8 GT tested by *Autocar* in 1972 and (breaking my rule about sources) those published in *Autosport* for a 'Downtonised' MGC tested by John Bolster in 1968. There has been no need to quote separate figures for cars sold in North America, as cars sold there had virtually the same power output and performance. I checked this very carefully in the case of the MGC, which was introduced to the USA just after the first exhaust-emission regulations had come into force, and I found that the necessary engine changes had made no difference to the performance.

The assembly of these figures, side by side and magazine-versus-magazine, as it were, raises all sorts of questions. First, however, to the performance figures themselves, given in Table E.1.

Notes

Twin-Cam Although *Autocar* and *Motor* were provided with sister cars by BMC, there was a considerable difference in their performance. A comparison of acceleration increments in top gear shows that the *Autocar* car was considerably slower up to 60mph, and rather faster above that speed.

216

Table E.1. *Performance figures*

Car	MGA Twin-Cam Tourer	MGA Twin-Cam Tourer	MGC Tourer o/d	MGC Tourer o/d	MGC GT Auto	MGC Tourer Downton Stage 2	MGB GT V8 o/d	MGB GT V8 o/d	MGB V8 Costello o/d
Mean maximum speed (mph)	113	113	120	118*	116	130 Plus	124*	125*	128
Axle Ratio	4.3	4.3	3.31	3.31	3.31	3.31	3.07	3.07	3.07
Acceleration (sec);									
0-30mph	4.3	2.6	4.0	3.6	4.4	3.4	2.8	2.9	2.8
0-40mph	6.9	4.4	5.6	5.1	6.2	4.8	4.3	4.3	4.4
0-50mph	9.4	7.3	7.6	7.6	8.2	6.5	6.4	5.9	5.9
0-60mph	13.3	9.1	10.0	10.0	10.9	8.2	8.6	7.7	7.8
0-70mph	17.3	12.3	13.8	13.7	14.6	11.0	11.8	10.5	10.8
0-80mph	22.5	16.2	18.0	17.7	18.8	13.9	15.1	13.0	13.6
0-90mph	30.0	24.6	23.1	22.6	26.3	—	19.0	17.3	17.3
0-100mph	41.1	40.3	29.3	30.1	35.8	22.1	25.3	23.4	22.0
0-110mph	—	—	40.9	—	—	—	35.6	32.5	29.9
Standing ¼-mile (sec)	18.6	18.1	17.7	17.6	18.2	16.5	16.4	15.8	15.8
Direct top gear (sec):									
10-30mph	—	—	11.1	—	—**	8.2	7.5	—	—
20-40mph	11.0	10.7	9.6	10.3	6.9	7.5	6.8	6.4	6.7
30-50mph	10.2	9.7	9.1	9.4	8.1	7.8	6.5	6.2	5.8
40-60mph	10.5	8.8	10.0	10.8	9.6	8.5	6.6	6.2	5.9
50-70mph	11.7	9.4	10.7	11.7	10.7	9.0	6.8	6.3	6.4
60-80mph	11.7	13.9	11.1	11.9	11.7	—	7.4	6.6	6.9
70-90mph	13.6	15.2	12.8	12.5	13.9	—	8.3	7.6	7.4
80-100mph	18.7	23.1	15.4	14.6	16.4	—	10.3	9.8	9.7
90-110mph	—	—	18.3	—	—	—	14.8	—	14.0
Overall mpg	21.8	22.2	17.5	19.3	19.0	22.5	23.4	19.8	18.8
Kerb weight (lb)	2156	2184	2477	2486	2615	—	2387	2374	2292
Test first published	1958	1958	1967	1967	1968	1968	1973	1973	1972
	Autocar	Motor	Autocar	Motor	Autocar	Autosport	Autocar	Motor	Autocar

* Denotes maximum speed achieved in overdrive top.
** Denotes top range of automatic transmission, but not in kickdown.

Motor's car was considerably faster off the mark, and through the gears, so much so that one questions the health of *Autocar*'s car, or the driving methods used by their testers. Even though they commented on wet testing conditions in the text of the report, there is a huge difference—4.2 seconds—in the time taken to sprint to 60mph, which increased to 6.3 seconds in the 0–80mph time.

On the other hand, *Autocar*'s car was significantly more economical at steady-speed consumption checks (not shown in my table) than was the *Motor* car.

All this makes me suspect that the *Autocar* car was either running on different carburettor/ignition timing settings, or that it was not achieving full throttle during the performance tests. Whatever the reason, I think we must assume that the *Motor* figures are more representative of the MGA Twin-Cam in normal healthy condition.

However, here is something else to add confusion to the equation. The Twin-Cam's nominal power-weight ratio was 112bhp/ton, while that of the MGC was 131bhp/ton, and yet in the top-gear figures which do not rely on driver skill this is hardly borne out by the figures, which are to the advantage of the Twin-Cam up to about 70mph!

MGC Here there was very little difference between the figures published by *Autocar* and *Motor*. However, it is significant that both cars achieved their best maximum speed in overdrive top. *Autocar*'s 120mph was achieved at 5,450rpm in direct top gear and at 4,450rpm in overdrive top gear. This certainly suggests that cars equipped with overdrive were overgeared, and it probably means that the 1969 model cars, which had an axle ratio of 3.7:1 when fitted with overdrive, were not only faster through the gears, but probably had a slightly higher maximum speed. However, no authoritative tests of such cars were ever carried out, so this must purely be an engineer's conjecture.

Only *Autocar* tested an automatic-transmission car, which was a GT derivative. In this case the gearing proved to be just about right, and the very creditable 116mph maximum speed was achieved at 5,250rpm. As expected, too, the automatic transmission car's acceleration from rest proved to be slightly less spectacular than that of manual transmission cars, though in average day-to-day use it is doubtful if anyone noticed.

The MGC tourer modified by Downton was tested by John Bolster in *Autosport* in November 1968, and it may be significant that his figures are also those quoted by Downton in their advertising literature. This, incidentally, was the Downton Stage 2 conversion, as fitted to a few University Motors cars in 1969 and 1970, and it clearly made a great difference to the breathing and revving capabilities of a much maligned engine. As an ex-professional road tester myself, however, I must confess to some doubts about these figures. The top-gear figures, though better than those for the standard car, are not nearly as good as those recorded in later years for the MGB GT V8. How, then, can we reconcile the fact that the sprint acceleration figures *are* as good as those for a V8?

218

Another point which amuses me is that Downton proudly claimed 149bhp (nett) for their Stage 2 conversion. What price, therefore, BMC's 'standard' rating of 145bhp (nett)? Either BMC were always telling tall stories, or Downton were being unduly modest—and I have never yet known a tuning firm to under-sell their capabilities.

MGB GT V8 In the case of the V8s tested by *Motor* and *Autocar* at the time of the launch, there was only a limited difference in capabilities. A study of top-gear increments suggests that the *Motor* car had a slightly more powerful engine; the increments are about 6 per cent faster overall, which suggests that the *Motor* car had about 10lb ft extra torque throughout.

This, now, is where I lose some friends. Even the briefest possible look at the figures shows that the V8 in standard trim was *much* more lively than the MGC. The MGC enthusiasts, I know, will state that it should indeed be so, because of the V8's much larger engine and massive increase in torque. The weight advantage to the MGB GT V8 is of the order of about 4 per cent, but it was inflicted by 6 per cent higher gearing overall (in terms of mph/1,000rpm figures), so this was effectively nullified.

A look at the top-gear increments proves the mighty torque of the modified Rover V8 engine, and shows that the 137bhp and 193lb ft torque (DIN) ratings of the MGB GT V8 must have been considerably more lusty than the 145bhp and 170lb ft torque (nett) ratings of the MGC. Unfortunately there is no accurate way of converting BMC 'nett' figures to DIN ratings. My own guess, however, made on the assumption that stopwatches do not lie, is that the V8 engine had up to 50 per cent more torque than the MGC unit throughout the speed range.

It is very interesting to note where and how the *Autocar*'s Costello V8—a straight conversion of an MGB GT, using a 150bhp (DIN) Rover 3500 engine, and weighing 90lb less than an 'official' Abingdon MGB GT V8—was faster than the factory model. In top gear it was only significantly quicker below 70mph, and by using all the gears (and the wider ratios of the MGB gearbox) it only began to pull away above that figure. Its maximum speed of 128mph, incidentally, was achieved in direct top gear, at an engine speed of 5,600rpm, whereas factory V8s habitually were fastest in overdrive.

I hope that this Appendix will answer every argument about the performance of Twin-Cams, MGCs and MGB GT V8s, and that it will allow the followers of each model to settle their friendly arguments in a civilised manner.

Acknowledgements

No book which sets out to survey the life and times of three such 'classic' MG sports cars could possibly have been written without a great deal of help, information, and advice from other MG experts. I would like, therefore, to mention those friends and colleagues who combined to make the job much easier.

For their personal involvement in the preservation of the Twin-Cam, MGC, and MGB GT V8 models—Peter Wood, Derek and Pearl McGlen, and Peter Laidler respectively. No-one else, certainly not the service staff of BL Cars at Unipart, knows as much about these cars as they do.

Geoff Allen of Abingdon, for his personal recollection of MGB GT V8 production, and for providing statistics.

Peter Mitchell (managing director), and Anders Clausager (archivist) for their help in making all manner of statistical material available at BL Heritage.

Hugh Bishop and Christine Crampton, for helping to find new photographs; John Cooper, of BL Photographic Department, Cowley, for previously providing so many other MG pictures.

Marcus Chambers, for his recollection of Twin-Cam prototype days; Richard Langworth—my personal North American connection; Warren Allport of *Autocar*—the invaluable guardian of everything historical in Britain's oldest motoring magazine.

Lastly, to the editors and staff of *Autocar*, *Motor*, and *Autosport*, for putting so many things in perspective when the cars were new, and for providing the independent comparisons needed to set the cars in their proper places on the motoring scene. And—of course—to *Thoroughbred & Classic Cars*, not only for bringing the MGC story more impartially up to date in 1977, 1978 and 1979, but for being the magazine which originally sparked off the great 'classic car' movement at the beginning of the 1970s.

Index

Note Mention of MG sports cars occurs so often in these pages that, except for some prototypes and special models, I have made no attempt to index them at all. References in **bold** type refer to pictorial mentions.